Two Moral Interludes:
The Pride of Life and *Wisdom*

MIDDLE ENGLISH TEXTS SERIES

GENERAL EDITOR
Russell A. Peck, University of Rochester

ASSOCIATE EDITOR
Alan Lupack, University of Rochester

ASSISTANT EDITOR
John H. Chandler, University of Rochester

ADVISORY BOARD

The Middle English Texts Series is designed for classroom use. Its goal is to make available to teachers and students texts that occupy an important place in the literary and cultural canon but have not been readily available in student editions. The series does not include those authors, such as Chaucer, Langland, or Malory, whose English works are normally in print in good student editions. The focus is, instead, upon Middle English literature adjacent to those authors that teachers need in compiling the syllabuses they wish to teach. The editions maintain the linguistic integrity of the original work but within the parameters of modern reading conventions. The texts are printed in the modern alphabet and follow the practices of modern capitalization, word formation, and punctuation. Manuscript abbreviations are silently expanded, and *u/v* and *j/i* spellings are regularized according to modern orthography. Yogh (3) is transcribed as *g*, *gh*, *y*, or *s*, according to the sound in Modern English spelling to which it corresponds; thorn (þ) and eth (ð) are transcribed as *th*. Distinction between the second person pronoun and the definite article is made by spelling the one *thee* and the other *the*, and final *-e* that receives full syllabic value is accented (e.g., *charité*). Hard words, difficult phrases, and unusual idioms are glossed on the page, either in the right margin or at the foot of the page. Explanatory and textual notes appear at the end of the text, often along with a glossary. The editions include short introductions on the history of the work, its merits and points of topical interest, and brief working bibliographies.

This series is published in association with the University of Rochester.

Medieval Institute Publications is a program of
The Medieval Institute, College of Arts and Sciences

 WESTERN MICHIGAN UNIVERSITY

TWO MORAL INTERLUDES:
THE PRIDE OF LIFE AND *WISDOM*

Edited by
David N. Klausner

TEAMS • Middle English Texts Series

MEDIEVAL INSTITUTE PUBLICATIONS
Western Michigan University
Kalamazoo

Library of Congress Cataloging-in-Publication Data

Pride of life.
 Two moral interludes : The pride of life and Wisdom / edited by David N. Klausner.
    p. cm. -- (Middle English texts)
 Includes bibliographical references.
 ISBN 978-1-58044-134-6 (pbk. : alk. paper)
1. Mysteries and miracle-plays, English. 2. Christian ethics--Drama. 3. Moralities,
English. I. Klausner, David N. II. Wisdom. III. Title.
 PR1261.M33P75 2008
 822'.2--dc22
                    2008015745

ISBN 978-1-58044-134-6

CONTENTS

ACKNOWLEDGMENTS

There are plenty of people to thank for their help in producing this edition. First, I owe a substantial debt to the cast of my 1991 production of *Wisdom* for challenging many of my assumptions about the play, to Otto Gründler for inviting me to produce it in the first place, and to Milla Cozart Riggio who, as dramaturge, pressed me to read the play in a more nuanced fashion. More recently, Russell Peck has been a continual source of support and advice, while Sandy Johnston read and commented on the whole volume. Juliana Dresvina and Richard Pollard assisted in the transcription of passages from Gonville and Caius College, Cambridge, MS. 140/80, and Abby Ann Young checked the Latin translations. The complex task of formatting the volume was in the hands of Leah Haught, and the manuscript and explanatory notes were reviewed by Kristi Castleberry. Alan Lupack of the Robbins Library and Patricia Hollahan at Medieval Institute Publications gave the completed volume its final review.

I am grateful to the librarians of the Folger Library, the Bodleian Library, the British Library, and the Master and Fellows of Gonville and Caius College, Cambridge, for permission to publish extracts of manuscripts in their care. Thanks are also due to Thomas H. Bestul for permission to quote in Appendix 1 from his TEAMS edition of Walter Hilton's *Scale of Perfection* (2000). Finally, it is a pleasure to acknowledge the generous support given to the Middle English Text Series by the National Endowment for the Humanities.

 **INTRODUCTION**

The surviving morality plays, or moral interludes, as they were generally known to their contemporaries, comprise a group of five texts from the late fourteenth to the early sixteenth centuries: *The Pride of Life, The Castle of Perseverance, Mankind, Wisdom,* and *Everyman.* Each of these plays deals allegorically with the life of man and his struggle against sin, and their structure is for the most part based on a sequence of temptation, fall, and redemption. Scholars have been hesitant to call this group of plays a genre, since each play differs from the others in substantial ways. *The Castle of Perseverance,* for example, describes the whole ontology of man, opening before his birth and ending after his death with his judgment before the throne of God. *Everyman,* in contrast, deals only with the final journey towards death. The group of plays is held together, however, by their consistent use of allegorical figures, by their use (in most cases) of a central representative human figure (variously called Mankind, Everyman, or Humanum Genus), and by their personification of the forces of good and evil which act upon him. Some of the plays (*Mankind, Wisdom*) require considerable theatrical resources and skill, sufficient to imply that they may have been intended for professional performance; *The Castle of Perseverance,* on the other hand, with its large cast of thirty-six players, must have been written for nonprofessional players or for a mixed group of professionals and nonprofessionals.[1]

The background to these plays lies in part in the allegorization of both good and evil which found its earliest expression in the *Psychomachia* of the late fourth-century poet Aurelius Clemens Prudentius. This poem describes a battle for the soul of man in which seven evil characteristics (Idolatry, Lust, Wrath, Pride, Indulgence, Greed, Discord) are pitted against seven virtues (Faith, Chastity, Patience, Humility, Sobriety, Good Works, Concord). Since the battle takes place within the mind of man, there is no representative human figure. Prudentius' allegorical mode was immensely popular throughout the Middle Ages, and became one of the primary models for the allegorization of human characteristics, leading eventually to such texts as the *Roman de la Rose* of Guillaume de Lorris and Jean de Meun, as well as Robert Grosseteste's *Chasteau d'Amour.* The second impetus behind the morality plays can be seen in the canon *Omnis utriusque sexus* of the Fourth Lateran Council (1215), which confirmed and elaborated earlier legislation and tradition requiring annual confession of all Christians, thus laying the ground for one of the most extensive educational programs in the history of the world. Faced with the necessity not only of educating the priesthood in the technical aspects and methodology of confession and penance but also of explaining to the laity the taxonomy

---

[1] For the possibility of mixed professional and nonprofessional casts for large plays, see Johnston, "Parish Playmaking," pp. 326–27.

of sins, allegory — the personification of individual sins, virtues, personal characteristics, or abstract qualities — was quickly adopted as an effective tool.

It is easy, however, to overestimate the importance of both these influences. The *Psycho-machia* provided only the most general model of an allegorical battle, while the nature of sin as presented in these plays was both well-known and orthodox, so the plays' purpose is less educational than, as Pamela M. King describes it, "to confirm and to celebrate rather than to argue."[2] From the late fifteenth century, the form and structure of the morality play was adapted in a variety of new directions, giving rise to a genre now most commonly known as the "Tudor interlude."[3] Where the morality play takes as its subject the whole moral life of man, the Tudor interludes focus on specific aspects of this life: e.g., the political (Skelton's *Magnyfycence*, Bale's *King Johan*), educational (*Wyt and Science*), or social (*Youth, Hick Scorner*).

The frequent use in the morality plays of a "Vice" figure distinguished from the allegorized sins, such as Backbiter in *The Castle of Perseverance*, Mischief and the three Worldlings in *Mankind*, and Lucifer in *Wisdom*, has been seen as influencing Shakespeare's Falstaff and Iago as well as Marlowe's Mephistopheles.[4] Indeed, for many years this possible influence on the canonical plays of the Elizabethan theater represented the sole interest in the morality plays. Those days are now past, and performances of all of these plays (with the exception of the fragmentary *Pride of Life*) have shown them to be highly effective vehicles for moral thought based on a keen understanding of the potential of allegory as a technique for the concrete representation of abstract ideas.

THE PRIDE OF LIFE

Although the date of the play now known as *The Pride of Life* has not been established with certainty, there is no question that it is the earliest of the surviving morality plays. The text of the play was written on one side of a parchment account roll from the Priory of the Holy Trinity in Dublin, where it appears on the back of the accounts for 30 June 1343 to 5 January 1344. Since the play is fitted into the blank spaces around the accounts, this would provide an earliest possible date for its composition. For reasons which will shortly become apparent, it is difficult to date the play with any precision, and a date as late as the "first half of the fifteenth century" has been proposed.[5] This is perhaps a bit extreme, and a date towards the end of the fourteenth century seems more likely.

The text of the play is incomplete and it seems certain that a second leaf containing the missing portion of the play was lost at some time in its history. The whole surviving portion of the manuscript was destroyed in June 1922, when the Four Courts building in Dublin, in which the manuscript had been placed along with others belonging to the canons of Christ Church, Dublin, was blown up. Fortunately, a transcription had been made of the play in 1891 by James Mills, deputy keeper of the Public Records. Mills published his transcription, along with a photographic facsimile of part of the roll, made by a zinc-based photographic method. This photograph and Mills' transcription are now the only surviving records of the original text. The photograph is not terribly clear, but it does allow a comparison between the manu-

---

[2] King, "Morality Plays," p. 243.

[3] See especially Craik, *Tudor Interlude*.

[4] See B. Spivack, *Shakespeare and the Allegory of Evil*, and Bevington, *From 'Mankind' to Marlowe*.

[5] Davis, *Non-Cycle Plays and Fragments*, p. lxxxv.

script and Mills' transcription, indicating clearly that his text is quite accurate — an important point, given the very sloppy way in which the original had been written. The text (as it survived in 1891) was written in eight blocks in blank spaces on the roll, these eight parts comprising lines 1–38, 39–126, 127–60, 161–96, 197–234, 235–326, 327–416, and 415–502. Some text appears to have been lost in the breaks between lines 126–27 and 326–27, and lines 415–16 were written twice, in each of the last two sections. Whatever text would have followed line 502 was lost before Mills transcribed it.

Fortunately, like many other medieval plays, *The Pride of Life* begins with a set of banns, a versified advertisement preceding the play proper.[6] In some cases, like *The Castle of Perseverance*, the banns were intended to precede the play by some days, perhaps as much as a week; in *The Pride of Life* they provide an introduction immediately preceding the play itself. These banns (lines 1–112) summarize the action of the play, and from them it is possible to reconstruct the action of the missing text, although only in a general way, and with many questions left unanswered.

Although the outline of the action follows the typical structure of sin and redemption, there are many differences between *The Pride of Life* and the morality plays of the fifteenth century. The central character is a king, rather than a clearly representative human figure. He is identified in the play as "Rex Vivus" — "King Life" or "The King of Life" — an epithet which may indicate that he is in fact intended to represent mankind as a whole.[7] Unusually among the morality plays (*Mankind* is the only other example), *The Pride of Life* is concerned with only one of the Seven Deadly Sins. Rex Vivus' sin is pride, and his royal status may have been chosen as appropriate to a prideful character. Nor does his temptation and fall into sin form a part of the action of the play; Rex Vivus is already full of pride at the opening of the play, delighting in the kind of bombast familiar from the biblical plays in such characters as Herod and Pilate. The king proclaims to the audience:

King ic am, kinde of kingis ikorre,	*descended from famous kings*
Al the worlde wide to welde at my wil;	*control*
Nas ther never no man of woman iborre	*born*
Ogein me withstonde that I nold him spille. (lines 121–24)	*Against; could not; destroy*

This stanza sets up the action of the play, for it is not "man of woman iborre" whom the king is to meet in battle but Death himself, as his pride (and his reliance on his two bodyguards, Health and Strength) leads him to challenge Death to a fight. There is no overt personification of pride, since the king has already fallen into the sin; virtue is represented by his wife, the queen, and the bishop, both of whom attempt to talk him out of his foolhardy challenge. The king's messenger, Mirth, seems positioned to occupy the position of a tempter figure or Vice, such as are found in many of the later moralities, but temptation is not a part of the play's action, and Mirth acts as no more than a messenger.

---

[6] Banns are also found preceding *The Castle of Perseverance*, the Chester plays, and the N-Town plays. Banns are also seen in other contexts; the reciting of banns was a required preliminary announcement of an impending marriage, and one example survives of banns advertising the arrival of a touring doctor, listing the ailments he is prepared to cure. See Voigts, "Fifteenth-Century English Banns."

[7] On the kingship of every individual see Gower's *Confessio Amantis*, Book 8.

The queen points out to Rex Vivus that Death overcomes all men, but he ignores her advice to fear God, supported in his pride by Health, Strength, and Mirth. Summoned by the queen, the bishop delivers a homily on the sorry state of the world (derived from a well-known poem, "The Abuses of the Age"), warning the king to think on his end. The king reacts in anger, and the surviving text comes to an abrupt end as Mirth is sent off to issue a challenge to Death. From this point on we must rely on the banns to fill in the rest of the play. Death kills Rex Vivus, whose sin of pride is thus repaid, and his soul is taken off by "the fendis" (line 96). The king's soul appears to be saved, however, as the banns explain the intercession of the Virgin, whose prayers will be taken into account as the soul is weighed in judgment. The banns do not indicate whether the Virgin does in fact intercede on the king's behalf as a part of the play, whether she or the fiends appear on stage, whether her intercession is successful, or whether her intervention is motivated by the prayers of the queen and the bishop. It seems quite likely that all of these elements combined to provide a dramatic conclusion to the play, though the state of the text does not allow us to be certain.

The play is clearly intended for "place and scaffold" staging, with the bulk of the action taking place on the scaffolds. At least two of these seem to be required, one each for the king and the bishop; other scaffolds (for Heaven and Hell, perhaps, or for Death) have been suggested, but are not necessary on the basis of the text as we have it. The king's scaffold at least would also need a curtained booth of some kind, since he asks his bodyguard Strength to "draw the cord," and the following stage direction indicates that he is enclosed in a curtained structure ("*clauso tentorio*"). Some of the action would have taken place in the "place" or "platea," the undifferentiated space at ground level between the scaffolds through which Mirth would move to issue the challenge to Death.[8] Control over the "place" must be constantly negotiated with the audience, who may very well be in the way of movement, and Mirth's explanation to them of his errand at the close of the surviving portion of the play is just such a speech of spatial negotiation. Mirth's lines are mirrored in both the morality plays and some of the biblical plays (notably the N-Town plays) when characters tell the audience to get out of the way. Clearly many more occasions in which a character must lay claim to a space are not directly reflected in the lines, but would have depended on the specific occasion and the distribution of audience. Such a situation is also implied by Jean Fouquet's minature of *The Martyrdom of St. Apollonia*, where spectators are seated on many of the acting areas which are not at the moment in use.[9]

WISDOM

With the exception of *Everyman*, which survives only in printed sources, *Wisdom* (also known as *Mind, Will, and Understanding*) is the only one of the morality plays to come down to us in more than one copy. A complete manuscript of the play is found in the Macro Manuscript, named after an eighteenth-century owner, the Rev. Cox Macro, and now in the Folger Library, Washington, DC. The manuscript also contains *The Castle of Perseverance* and *Mankind*. A second copy of the first 752 lines of *Wisdom* also survives in MS Digby 133, now in the Bodleian Library, Oxford. Milla Cozart Riggio has established the very great likelihood that

---

[8] This assumes that Norman Davis' expansion of the incomplete stage direction at line 470 ("Et eat pla<team.>") is correct (*Non-Cycle Plays and Fragments*, p. 104).

[9] A good reproduction of the miniature can be found in *Hours of Etienne Chevalier*, plate 45.

the Macro text of the play was copied from the Digby manuscript, though the possibility that both were copied from a now-lost text cannot be ruled out.[10]

The play differs from the other moralities in its characters, its structure, and its theological content. The central human figure is represented here not by one character but by nine — Anima, the human soul; her five attendant senses; and her three human faculties of Mind, Will, and Understanding. The play is structured around the marriage of Anima to Wisdom, who is explicitly presented as an avatar of Christ, and around Lucifer's efforts to destroy this marriage through the seduction of her human faculties. Within this overarching structure, the action of the play proceeds in four sections; although this division is not indicated in the manuscripts, it seems clear enough that at least one editor has printed the play divided into four scenes.[11] The first of these scenes explains (in a format clearly derived from the late medieval sermon) the relationship between Wisdom and Anima. This relationship is also presented visually through the very elaborate costuming described in the play's expansive stage directions. The description of Anima dressed in white (indicative of her purity) with a black over-mantle (symbolizing original sin), as well as her status as potential bride to Christ, are derived primarily from the writings of the German theologian Heinrich Suso, whose *Orologium Sapientiae* was translated into English earlier in the fifteenth century as *The Seuene Poyntes of Trewe Loue and Euerlastynge Wisdome*, of which relevant passages are printed in Appendix 1.

The second "section" of the play involves Lucifer's very successful seduction of the three faculties or Mights: Mind, Will, and Understanding. The three Mights appear to be presented as cloistered monks, and Lucifer's argument is designed to convince them of the superiority of the active life in the world over the contemplative life of the cloister. Much of Lucifer's argument is derived from Walter Hilton's *Epistle on the Mixed Life*, the relevant passages of which are also printed in Appendix 1. Lucifer adopts Hilton's point (following Ecclesiastes 3:1) that all things have their appropriate times. He subtly twists Hilton's statement that we must sometimes act with Martha in governing the household with work, and sometimes with Mary in setting aside the business of the world to worship God; he also uses Hilton's description of Christ's life as a combination of the active and the contemplative modes.

The third part of the play demonstrates in the most flamboyant manner the fallen state of the three Mights, who have changed their monastic habits for the dress of fashionable gallants. They have each changed their names, and they call in their followers for a series of masque dances, accompanied onstage by minstrels. Each group is dressed in the livery of its master, described in stage directions as explicit as those for Wisdom and Anima's costumes. Mind has become Maintenance (a complex idea involving the purchase of followers' support; the closest modern equivalent would be "graft"); he is followed by Indignation, Sturdiness, Malice, Rashness, Wretchedness, and Discord. Their livery is comprised of several images of force — red beards, lions rampant on their badges, and a weapon in the hands of each; their dance music is played aggressively on trumpets. Understanding has become Perjury, and his followers (Wrong, Slight, Doubleness, Falsehood, Rapine, and Deceit) are dressed as jurors. As he introduces them, Understanding notes that the "jurors in one hood bear two faces," which likely implies that they wear two-faced masks. They are accompanied by a bagpipe.

---

[10] Riggio, *Play of Wisdom*, pp. 6–18.

[11] Eccles, *Macro Plays*.

Will's metamorphosis into Lechery appears to involve some serious gender-bending: his followers are six women, three of them disguised as (male) gallants, the other three dressed as women. Their dance is accompanied by a hornpipe. This third dance breaks down into a fight among the three faculties indicating the level of discord into which they have fallen. The fight is settled by Will, and the three discuss their next moves — Understanding/Perjury and Mind/Maintenance will haunt the law courts and the government in order to take bribes, while Will/Lechery intends to head for the nearest brothel. As they plot their strategies in language which suggests substantial understanding of the law on the part of the audience, Wisdom returns to rebuke them for their fall. They pay little attention until Anima reappears, "fouler than a fiend," with a pack of "small boys" dressed as devils who run out from under her mantle. The three Mights repent their sins and the devils are driven from the stage. Anima, Mind, Will, and Understanding leave the stage to seek mercy, as Anima sings a penitential passage from the Lamentations of Jeremiah. Wisdom, alone on stage, presents a sermon to the audience on the subject of the nine things which most please God, a text well-known in both Latin and English versions, sometimes attributed to Richard Rolle (a closely related Latin version is printed in Appendix 1).

Anima returns, accompanied by her full retinue of faculties and senses, all of them costumed as in the opening of the play with the addition of crowns. She describes her faults, both in her "inward wits" (the three faculties) and her "outward wits" (her five senses), pointing out that since her own contrition is not sufficient for redemption, she must now ask Wisdom for God's grace. His reply, the most dramatic moment of the play, describes the pain of Anima's fall as equal to that of the Crucifixion, which pain has now been remedied through Anima's penance and the gift of grace. In passages again based on Walter Hilton's *Scale of Perfection* (see Appendix 1), the three Mights indicate their own participation in Anima's redemption, and she closes the play, concluding that human perfection can only be achieved through the avoidance of sin and the renewal of grace.

Unusually among the morality plays, *Wisdom* raises significant issues of gender. Anima herself is clearly feminine, and is presented as a bride of Christ; her attributes, however, include not only her five interior senses, represented by the five (female) virgins, but also her three clearly masculine mights or powers, Mind, Will, and Understanding. To a certain extent, these mixed-gender attributes can be seen to reflect the gender ambiguity inherent in Christian theology, especially as it is seen in the Canticles — a major source for the play. The extreme cross-dressing of the third masque dance, however, presents gender ambiguities in a manner which can be seen as highly subversive. An important question raised in recent discussions of the play is the extent to which this subversive quality extends to gender roles elsewhere in the play.[12]

No performance history for the play survives, though it is evident from the extensive stage directions, as well as the marginal directions at lines 685 and 785, that the play was intended for performance. Some limited information can, however, be gleaned from the playtext and its manuscript concerning its performance. First, the large cast of actors, singers, and dancers, as well as the very elaborate costuming described by the stage directions, indicate sponsorship by a very wealthy person or institution. A monk by the name of Hyngham wrote two lines of verse at the end of the play as the owner of the book, and he has been identified as Thomas

---

[12] See, especially, C. Spivack, "Feminine vs. Masculine," pp. 137–44; Clark, Kraus, and Sheingorn, "'Se in what stat thou doyst indwell,'" pp. 43–57; and Nisse, *Defining Acts*, pp. 125–47.

Hengham, a member of the monastic community at the abbey of Bury St. Edmunds, Norfolk, in the 1470s. Bury was a notably wealthy house, and was visited by royalty on numerous occasions. The playtext itself also provides some useful information: the discussion of the advantages of the mixed life over the contemplative life which forms the basis of Lucifer's seduction of the three Mights implies an audience for whom the theological status of the mixed life would be of interest. This need not have necessarily been a monastic audience; ownership of books on the subject shows that thoughtful members of the laity were also interested in the topic.[13] The lives of vice which the three Mights adopt after their seduction are strongly rooted in the world of the London law courts, and an understanding of this part of the play would require some competency in the law on the part of the audience, as well as an understanding of the most significant law-and-order problems of the period. Again, this does not necessarily imply an audience of lawyers, since training in the law was seen as an appropriate preliminary to the administration of an estate, and in the litigious society of the late fifteenth century knowledge of the law was widespread among the gentry. Monks and lawyers may well have been among the spectators for *Wisdom*, but the primary requirement for the audience would be a substantial degree of education. A mixed audience at the abbey of Bury St. Edmund's would certainly be a possibility, but a wealthy secular household would also be a likely venue for the play's performance, and households in the vicinity of Bury which might have housed the play would include those of John Morton, bishop of Ely, the Howard dukes of Norfolk, or the de la Pole dukes of Suffolk.[14]

THE TEXT

The manuscript texts have been lightly modernized to normalize the scribe's inconsistent use of u/w and i/j. Some consistency has also been introduced in the spelling of ambiguous words, so the second person singular pronoun always appears as "thee" and the definite article as "the"; "of" and "off" are likewise regularized, and all roman numerals are spelled out. Clear scribal errors are corrected without comment, and passages in the damaged portions of *The Pride of Life* which have been reconstructed conjecturally are indicated by square brackets. Most of these conjectures derive from the suggestions made by Norman Davis in his EETS edition of the play. Latin words and phrases in the text are translated in the notes.

---

[13] On the play's connections with the abbey of Bury St. Edmunds, see especially Riggio, "Staging of *Wisdom*," and Gibson, "Play of *Wisdom*," both in Riggio, *"Wisdom" Symposium*, as well as Gibson's *Theater of Devotion*, pp. 108–26.

[14] Morton was suggested as a possible patron for the play by Milton McC. Gatch, "Mysticism and Satire," pp. 342–62; the Howards and de la Poles were proposed by Alexandra F. Johnston, *"Wisdom and the Records"*; *Wisdom* as household drama is discussed by Suzanne Westfall, *Patrons and Performance*.

Manuscripts

The Pride of Life

Indexed as item 2741 in Boffey and Edwards, eds., *New Index of Middle English Verse*:
  • Dublin, Christ Church Cathedral, now destroyed; "partly available in facsimile in J. Mills, (Dublin, 1891)."

Editions and facsimiles:
Coldewey, John, ed. *Early English Drama: An Anthology*. New York: Garland, 1993.
Davis, Norman, ed. *Non-Cycle Plays and Fragments*. EETS s.s. 1. London: Oxford University Press, 1970.
———. *Non-Cycle Plays and the Winchester Dialogues*. Leeds: Leeds University Press, 1979.
Happé, Peter, ed. *Tudor Interludes*. Harmondsworth: Penguin, 1972.
Mills, James, ed. *The Account Roll of the Priory of the Holy Trinity, Dublin, 1337–1346, with the Middle English Moral Play "The Pride of Life."* Dublin: Royal Society of Antiquaries of Ireland, 1891.

Wisdom

Indexed as item 1440 in Boffey and Edwards, eds., *New Index of Middle English Verse*:
  • Folger MS V.a.354 (the Macro manuscript) *NIMEV*: Folger Shakespeare Library 5031
  • Bodleian Library MS Digby 133

Editions and facsimiles:
Baker, D. C., J. L. Murphy, and L. B. Hall, Jr., eds. *The Late Medieval Religious Plays of Bodleian MSS Digby 133 and E. Museo 160*. Oxford: Oxford University Press, 1982. [the text from the Digby manuscript]
Bevington, David, ed. *The Macro Plays: A Facsimile Edition with Facing Transcription*. New York: Johnson Reprint, 1972.
Coldewey, John, ed. *Early English Drama: An Anthology*. New York: Garland, 1993.
Eccles, Mark, ed. *The Macro Plays*. EETS o.s. 262. London: Oxford University Press, 1969.
Riggio, Milla Cozart, ed. *The Play of Wisdom: Its Texts and Contexts*. New York: AMS Press, 1998.
Walker, Greg, ed. *Medieval Drama*. Oxford: Blackwell, 2000.

THE PRIDE OF LIFE (REX VIVUS)

PROLOCUTOR Pees, and herkynt hal ifer,	*listen all together*
[Ric] and por, yong and hold,	*old*
Men and wemen that bet her,	*who are here*
Bot lerit and leut, stout and bold.	*Both educated; uneducated (lewd); strong*
5 Lordinges and ladiis that beth hende,	*at hand*
Herkenith al with mylde mode	*kindly disposition*
[How ou]re gam schal gyn and ende.	*play; begin*
Lorde us wel spede that sched his blode!	
Now stondith stil and beth hende,	*be attentive*
10 [And ter]yith al for the weder,	*stay (tarry); because of the weather*
[And] ye schal or ye hennis wende	*before you go hence*
Be glad that ye com hidir.	*here*
Here ye schullin here spelle	*shall hear a story*
Of mirth and eke of kare;	*also*
15 Herkenith and I wol you telle	
[How this our gam] schal fare.	*play; go*
[Of the Kyng of] Lif I wol you telle;	
[He stondith] first biffore	
[All men that beth] of flessch and fel	*skin*
20 [And of woman i]bore.	*born*
[He is, forsoth, ful] stronge to stond,	*truly*
[And is] bycomin of kinge,	*born of a royal line*
[Giveth] lawis in eche a londe,	
[And nis] dradd of no thinge.	*afraid*
25 [In] pride and likinge his lif he ledith,	*pleasure*
Lordlich he lokith with eye;	*Commandingly*
[Prin]ce and dukis, he seith, him dredith,	*fear him*
[He] dredith no deth for to deye.	*fears*
[He] hath a lady lovelich al at likinge,	*pleasure*
30 Ne may he of no mirth mene ne misse;	*complain about*

He seith in swetnisse he wol set his likinge
And bringe his bale boun into blisse.   *sorrow quickly to*

Knytis he hat cumlic   *handsome*
In bred and in leint;   *breadth; height*
35   Not I nevir non suc   *I have never known such*
Of stotey ney of strynt.   *bravery nor of strength*

Wat helpit to yilp mucil of his mit   *complain bitterly; power*
Or bost to mucil of his blys?   *too much*
[For] sorou may sit on is sit   *his seat*
40   [And] myrt[h m]ay he not miss.   *lack*

[Here ek is the] ladi of lond,   *also*
[The fa]inist a lord for to led;   *most beautiful*
[Glad] may he be for to stond
[And b]ehold that blisful bled.   *lovely creature*

45   [Tha]t ladi is lettrit in lor   *educated; wisdom*
As cumli becomit for a quen,   *fittingly*
And munit hir mac evirmor,   *reminds; husband always*
As a dar for dred him to ten.   *she dares; anger*

Ho bid him bewar or he smert,   *She; before; dies*
50   [F]or in his lond Det wol alend;   *Death; come*
[As] ho lovit him gostlic in hert   *loves; profoundly*
[Ho b]it him bewar of his hend.   *bids; ending*

[Ho] begynit to charp of char   *speak; care*
Thes wordis wytout lesing: *falsehood*
55   "Det dot not spar   *Death does*
Knytis, cayser, ne kyng.   *emperor*

Nou lord, lev thi likynd   *leave; pleasure*
Wyc bryngit the soul gret bal."   *Which; pain*
This answer ho had of the kyng;   *she*
60   "Ye, this a wommanis tal."   *idle speech*

The kyng hit ne toke not to hert
For hit was a womanis spec   *speech*
[And y]et hit mad him to smert   *feel pain*
[W]an him mit help no lec.   *When; might; doctor*

65   [The] quen yit can hir undirstond   *further*
Wat help thar mit be,   *might*
And sent aftir the bicop of the lond   *bishop*
For he chout mor than he.   *knew more than she*

He cham and precit al that he couthe,   *came; preached; could*
70   And warnit him hal of his hind;   *thoroughly; end*
      [H]it savrit not in the kyngis mout,   *It does not taste good in the king's mouth*
      Bot hom he bad him wynd.   *home; commanded; to go*

      Wan the bicop is tham wend   *gone*
      Fram that kene stryf   *bitter*
75   [To Det a me]ssenger than send   *Death; then sent*
      [Hat] the Kyng of Lif.   *Has*

      [For he] him wold do undirstond   *would cause him to understand*
      [That al] he may del and dit: *control; govern*
      [He] wold cum into his owin lond   *[Death] should come*
80   On him to kyt his mit.   *Upon him to show his power*

      Deth comith, he dremith a dredfful dreme —
      Welle aghte al carye;   *ought all to be afraid*
      And slow fader and moder and then heme: *slew; then [his] uncle*
      He ne wold none sparye.   *spare*

85   Sone after hit befel that Deth and Life
      Beth togeder itaken;   *Happen to come together*
      And ginnith and strivith a sterne strife   *begin; fierce struggle*
      The King of Life to wrake.   *ruin*

      With him drivith adoun to grounde,   *vigorously [Death] drives him*
90   He dredith nothing his knightis;   *[Death] fears not at all*
      And delith him depe dethis wounde
      And kith on him his mightis.   *manifests*

      Qwhen the body is doun ibroght
      The soule sorow awakith;
95   The bodyis pride is dere aboght,   *body's pride is dearly bought*
      The soule the fendis takith.   *devils seize*

      And throgh priere of Oure Lady mylde   *prayer*
      The soule and body schul dispyte;   *part ways (be in dispute)*
      Scho wol prey her son so mylde,
100   Godenisse scho wol qwyte.   *reward*

      The cors that nere knewe of care,   *body; never experienced grief*
      No more then stone in weye,   *than a stone in the road*
      Schal wit of sorow and sore care   *know*
      And thrawe betwene ham tweye.   *suffer between the two of them*

105   The soule theron schal be weye   *weighed*
      That the fendis have ikaghte;   *devils; caught*

And Oure Lady schal therfor preye
So that with her he schal be lafte.   *[the soul] shall remain*

Nou beith in pes and beith hende,   *rest in peace and be attentive*
110   And distourbith noght oure place,   *stage*
For this oure game schal gin and ende   *play; begin*
Throgh Jhesu Cristis swete grace.

        Rex Vivus incipiet sic dicendum: *The King of Life begins, speaking thus*

[**Rex**]   Pes, now, ye princis of powere so prowde,   *King*
Ye kingis, ye kempis, ye knightis ikorne,   *warriors; chosen*
115   Ye barons bolde, that beith me obowte;   *who attend me*
[Sem] schal yu my sawe, swaynis isworne.[1]

Squieris stoute, stondit now stille,
And lestenith to my hestis, I hote yu now her,   *orders; command; here*
Or I schal wirch yu wo with werkis of wil   *punish you with firm measures*
120   And doun schal ye drive, be ye never so dere.   *[be] driven; courageous*

King ic am, kinde of kingis ikorre,   *descended from famous kings*
Al the worlde wide to welde at my wil;   *control*
Nas ther never no man of woman iborre   *born*
Ogein me withstonde that I nold him spille.   *Against; could not; destroy*

125   Lordis of lond beith at my ledinge,   *command*
Al men schal abow in hal and in bowr;   *bow down in hall; private apartment*
. . . .

[**Regina**]   Baldli thou art mi bot,   *Queen; Assuredly; protector*
Tristili and ful treu;   *Faithfully*
Of al mi rast thou art rot,   *comfort; root*
130   I nil chong fer no new.   *will not change for*

Rex   Al in wel ic am biwent,   *gone*
May no grisful thing me grou;   *terrible; grieve*
Likyng is wyt me bilent,   *Pleasure; come to me*
Alyng is it mi behou.   *Altogether; benefit*

135   Strent and Hel, knytis kete,   *Strength and Health, bold knights*
[Douti], derrist in ded,   *Brave, boldest in deed*
Lok that for no thing ye let   *nothing hinder you*
Smartli to me sped.   *Quickly to attend me*

---

[1] *My speech shall [be] pleasing [to] you, [my] sworn retainers*

	Bringit wyt you brit brondis,	*bright swords*
140	Helmis brit and schen;	*Helmets; shining*
	For ic am lord ofir al londis	
	And that is wel isen.	*very clear*

PRIMUS MILES, FORTITUDO   *FIRST SOLDIER, STRENGTH*

	Lord, in truthe thou mit trist	*may trust [me]*
	Fethfuli to stond	
145	Thou mit liv as thee list,	*please*
	For wonschildis thu fond.	*defenders; have found*

	Ic am Strent, stif and strong,	*Strength, steadfast*
	Nevar is suc non,	*such a one*
	In al this world brod and long,	
150	Imad of blod and bon.	*Made*

	Hav no dout of no thing	
	That evir may befal;	
	Ic am Streynt thi derling	
	Flour of knitis al.	*Flower; knights*

SECUNDUS MILES, SANITAS   *SECOND SOLDIER, HEALTH*

155	King of Lif, that berist the croun,	*wears*
	As hit is skil and righte	*reasonable*
	I am Hele icom to toun,	*Health*
	Thi kind curteyse knighte.	

	Thou art lord of lim and life,	*body*
160	And king withouten ende;	
	Stif and strong and sterne in strif,	*Steadfast; unwavering*
	In londe qwher thou wende.	*where; go*

	Thou nast no nede to sike sore	*have not any need; sigh*
	For no thing on lyve;	
165	Thou schal lyve evermore:	
	Qwho dar with thee strive?	*Who*

REX   Strive? Nay, to me qwho is so gode?   *[compared] to me who*
          Hit were bot folye;
          Ther is no man that me dur bode   *dares threaten me with*
170   Any vileynye.

          Qwherof schuld I drede
          Qwhen I am King of Life?
          Ful evil schuld he spede
          To me that wroght strive.   *offers strife*

175   I schal lyve evermo
      And croun ber as kynge;   *wear*
      I ne may never wit of wo,   *know any woe*
      I lyve at my likinge.   *for my pleasure*

REGINA   Sire, thou saist as thee liste,   *wish*
180   Thou livist at thi wille;   *according to your*
      Bot somthing thou miste,   *omitted*
      And therfor hold thee stille.

      Thinke, thou haddist beginninge
      Qwhen thou were ibore;   *born*
185   And bot thou mak god endinge   *unless*
      Thi sowle is forlore.   *lost*

      Love God and Holy Chirche,
      And have of him som eye;   *them; fear*
      Fonde his werkis for to wirch   *Try; do*
190   And thinke that thou schal deye.   *be mindful*

REX   Douce dam, qwhi seistou so?   *Sweet lady; say you*
      Thou spekis noght as the sleye.   *wise*
      I schal lyve evermo
      For bothe two thin eye.   *your two eyes*

195   Woldistou that I were dede   *Do you wish I were dead*
      That thou might have a new?   *[So] you; new [husband]*
      Hore, the devil gird off thi hede   *Whore; strike off*
      Bot that worde schal thee rewe!   *regret*

REGINA   Dede, sire? Nay, God wote my wil,   *knows*
200   That ne kepte I noghte;   *That [thought]*
      Hit wolde like me full ille   *please*
      Were hit thareto broghte.   *brought to pass*

      [Yet] thogh thou be kinge
      Nede schalt have ende;   *Necessity; come at last*
205   Deth overcomith al thinge
      How-so-ever we wende.   *go*

REX   Ye, dam, thou hast wordis fale,   *many words*
      Hit comith thee of kinde;   *naturally*
      This nis bot women tale,   *nothing but women's talk*
210   And that I wol thee finde.   *show*

      I ne schal never deye
      For I am King of Life;

Deth is undir myne eye   *in awe of me*
And therfor leve thi strife.   *arguing*

215 Thou dost bot mak myn hert sore,
For hit nel noght helpe;   *will not*
I prey thee spek of him no more.
Qwhat wolte of him yelpe?   *brag*

REGINA Yilpe, sire? Ney, so mot I the;   *Brag; thrive*
220 I sigge hit noght therfore,   *said*
Bot kinde techith bothe thee and me,   *nature*
First qwhen we were bore,

For doute of Dethis maistri,   *fear; power*
To wepe and make sorowe;
225 Holy writ and prophecye   *scripture*
Therof I take to borowe.   *as evidence*

Therfor, qwhile ye have mighte
And the worlde at wille,
I rede ye serve God Almighte   *advise*
230 Bothe loude and stille.

This world is bot fantasye
And ful of trechurye;
Gode sire, for youre curteysye
Take this for no folye.

235 For, God wot the sothe,   *truth*
I ne sey hit for no fabil;   *fiction*
Deth wol smyte to thee,
In feith loke thou be stabil.   *steadfast*

REX Qwhat prechistou of Dethis might   *do you preach*
240 And of his maistrye?   *power*
He ne durst onis with me fight   *dares not once*
For his bothe eye.   *both his eyes*

Streinth and Hele, qwhat say ye,
My kinde korin knightis?   *gracious chosen*
245 Schal Deth be lord over me
And reve me of mightis?   *deprive*

I MILES Mi lord, so brouke I my bronde,   *as I wield my sword*
God that me forbede
That Deth schold do thee wronge
250 Qwhile I am in thi thede.   *country*

I wol withstonde him with strife
And make his sidis blede,
And tel him that thou art King of Life
And lorde of londe and lede.   *people*

II Miles   May I him onis mete   *once*
256   With this longe launce,
In felde other in strete,   *or*
I wol him give mischaunce.   *bad luck*

Rex   Ye, thes be knightis of curteisye
260   And doghti men of dede;   *brave*
Of Deth ne of his maistrie   *power*
Ne have I no drede.

Qwher is Mirth my messager,
Swifte so lefe on lynde?   *as a leaf on the lime tree*
265   He is a nobil bachelere   *young man*
That rennis bi the wynde.   *runs like*

Mirth and solas he can make   *comfort*
And ren so the ro;   *run like the roe deer*
Lightly lepe ovre the lake   *stream*
270   Qwher-so-ever he go.

Com and her my talente   *desire*
Anone and hy the blyve: *Quickly and hurry immediately*
Qwher any man, as thou has wente,   *Whether; wherever you have gone*
Dorst with me to strive?   *Dares*

Nuncius   King of Lif and lord of londe,   *Messenger*
276   As thou sittis on thi se   *seat*
And florresschist with thi bright bronde,   *sword*
To thee I sit on kne.   *I kneel*

I am Mirth, wel thou wost,   *know*
280   Thi mery messagere;
That wostou wel, withoute bost,   *you know*
Ther nas never my pere   *equal*

Doghtely to done a dede   *Bravely; do*
That ye have for to done,
285   Hen to Berewik upon Twede   *From here*
And com ogein ful sone;

Ther is nothing thee iliche   *equal*
In al this worlde wide

Of gold and silver and robis riche
290 And hei hors on to ryde.   *tall*

I have ben bothe fer and nere
In bataile and in strife;
Ocke ther was never thy pere,   *But; peer*
For thou art King of Life.

Rex Aha! Solas, now thou seist so,   *Comfort*
296 Thou miriest me in my mode;   *make merry; mind*
Thou schal, boy, ar thou hennis go   *before; hence*
Be avaunsyd, bi the Rode.   *promoted; Cross*

Thou schal have for thi gode wil
300 To thin avauncemente,   *As your promotion*
The castel of Gailispire on the Hil,
And the erldom of Kente.

Draw the cord, Sire Streynth,   *curtain string*
Rest I wol now take;
305 On erth in brede ne leynth
Ne was nere yet my make.   *never; equal*

Et tunc clauso tentorio dicet Regina secrete nuncio:[1]

Regina Messager, I pray thee nowe
For thi curteysye,
Go to the bisschop, for thi prowe,   *profit*
310 And byd him hydir to hye.   *hurry*

Bid him be ware before,
Sey him that he most preche;
My lord the King is ney lore   *almost lost*
Bot he wol be his leche.   *Unless*

315 Sey him that he wol leve noght   *believe*
That ever he schal deye;
He is in siche errour broghte   *such*
Of God stont him non eye.   *he has; fear*

Nuncius Madam, I make no tarying
320 With softe wordis mo;
For I am Solas, I most singe   *Comfort; must*
Overal qwher I go.   *Everywhere*

---

[1] *Then, having closed the curtain, the Queen speaks privately with the messenger*

Et cantat.   *And he sings*

      Sire Bisschop, thou sittist on thi se   *seat*
      With thi mitir on thi hevede;   *miter; head*
325 My lady the Qwen preyith thee
      Hit schold noght be bilevyd.   *neglected*

      . . . .

EPISCOPUS The world is now, so wo-lo-wo,   *BISHOP; alas*
      In suc bal ibound   *such evil*
      That dred of God is al ago   *gone*
330 And treut is go to ground.   *truth; laid low*

      Med is mad a demisman,   *Bribery; judge*
      Streyint betit the law;   *Strength overcomes*
      Geyl is mad a cepman   *Deceit; merchant*
      And truyt is don of dau.   *truth is put to death*

335 Wyt is now al trecri,   *treachery*
      Othis fals and gret;   *Oaths*
      Low is nou al lecuri   *Law; lechery*
      And corteysi is let.   *hindered*

      Play is now vileni,   *villainy*
340 Cildrin bet onlerit,   *are uneducated*
      Halliday is glotuny —   *Holy days*
      This lawis bet irerit.   *These; are established*

      Slet men bet bleynd   *Wise; blinded*
      And lokit al amis;   *see everything*
345 He bicomit onkynd   *They; unnatural*
      And that is reut, iwis.   *pity; truly*

      Frend may no man find
      Of fremit ne of sib;   *Unrelated nor related*
      The ded bet out of mind,   *are*
350 Gret sorw it is to lib.   *live*

      Thes ricmen bet reuthyles,   *pitiless*
      The por got to ground,   *are destroyed*
      And fals men bet schamles,   *are*
      The sot ic hav ifound.   *truth I*

355 It is wrong the ric knyt
      Al that the por dot;   *do*

Far that is sen day and nit   *Far and wide; seen*
Wosa wol sig sot.   *Whoso will speak truth*

360 Paraventur men halt me a fol   *Perhaps; consider*
     To sig that sot tal;   *speak that true tale*
     Thai farit as ficis in a pol —   *live like fish*
     The gret eteit the smal.   *eat*

     Ricmen spart for no thing   *spare*
     To do the por wrong;
365 Thai thingit not on hir ending   *think*
     Ne on Det that is so strong.   *Nor on Death*

     Nothir thai lovit God ne dredit   *Neither*
     Nother him no his lawis;   *nor*
     Touart hel fast him spedit   *Towards hell; hasten*
370 Ageins har ending-daws.   *Before their last days*

     Bot God of his godnis
     Gif ham gras to amend,   *Gives them grace*
     Into the delful derknys   *terrible*
     The got wytout hend.   *Which lasts*

375 Ther is dred and sorow
     And wo wytoutin wel;   *without*
     No man may othir borow   *rescue*
     Be ther nevir so fel.   *many*

     Ther ne fallit no maynpris,   *be available; bail*
380 Ne supersidias;   *(see note)*
     Thay he be kyng or iustis,   *Though; judge*
     He passit not the pas.   *passage (death's door)*

     Lord, that for his manhed
     And also for his god,   *goodness*
385 That for lov and not for dred
     Deit oppon the Rod,   *Died; Cross*

     Gif ou gras or lif to led   *Give you grace*
     That be your soulis to bot;   *For your souls' salvation*
     God of Hevin for his godhed
390 Lev that hit so mot. Amen.   *Permit; may be so*

     Tunc dicet regi: *Then he says to the king*

     Schir Kyng, thing uppon thin end   *Sir; think*
     And how that thou schalt dey,

Wat wey that thou schalt wend   *go*
Bot thou be bisey.   *Unless; take care*

395   And eke that thou art lenust man,   *also; very frail*
And haddist begyning,
And evirmor hav thout opon   *thought*
Thi dredful ending.   *fearful*

Thou schalt thing thanne —   *think (remember)*
400   And mac thee evir yar —   *make yourself; ready*
That Det is not the man   *Death; your servant*
For nothing thee wil spar.   *will spare you*

Thou schalt do dedis of rit   *justice*
And lernen Cristis lor,   *wisdom*
405   And lib in hevin-lit   *live; heaven's light*
To savy thi soul fro sor.   *save; pain*

REX   Wat! Bissop, byssop babler,   *What*
Schold Y of Det hav dred?   *Should I fear Death*
Thou art bot a chagler —   *windbag (jangler)*
410   Go hom thi wey, I red.   *advise*

Wat! com thou therfor hidir
Wit Deth me to afer?   *frighten*
That thou and he bot togidir   *both together*
Into the se scot wer.   *sea thrown*

415   Go hom, God gif thee sorow,   *give*
Thou wreist me in my mod.   *anger; mind*
War woltou prec tomorou?   *Where will you preach*
Thou nost ner, bi the Rod!   *don't know at all; Cross*

Troust thou I wold be ded   *Believe*
420   In mi yyng lif?   *young*
Thou lisst, screu, bolhed;   *lie, villain, idiot*
Evil mot thou thrive.

Wat schold I do at churg, wat?   *church*
Schir bisop, wostou er?   *do you know*
425   Nay, churc nis no wyl cat,   *wild*
Hit wol abid ther.   *stay*

I wool let car away,   *worry (care) [go] away*
And go on mi pleying.   *concentrate on*
To hontyng and to othir play
430   For al thi long prechyng.   *long-winded*

I am yyng, as thou mit se,
And hav no ned to char   *be worried*
The wyle the Quen and [mi me]iné   *While; retinue*
About me bet yar.   *are ready*

EPISCOPUS Thynk, Schir Kyng, one othir trist —   *Believe; otherwise*
436 That tyng misst son.   *will fail soon*
Thot thou lev now as the list,   *Though; live; you please*
Det wol cum rit son,   *very soon*

And give thee dethis wounde
440 For thin outrage;   *presumption*
Within a litil stounde   *short time*
Then artou but a page.   *servant*

Qwhen thou art graven on grene,   *buried*
Ther metis fleys and molde,   *come together flies and mold*
445 Then helpith litil, I wene,   *believe*
Thi gay croun of golde.

Sire Kyng, have goday,
Crist I you beteche.   *commend you to*
REX Fare wel, bisschop, thi way,
450 And lerne bet to preche.   *better*

        Hic adde.   *Here he leaves*

Now, mafay, hit schal be sene,   *by my faith*
I trow, yit to-daye,
Qwher Deth me durst tene   *dares trouble*
And mete in the waye.

455 Qwher artou, my messagere,
Solas bi thi name?
Loke that thou go fer and nere,
As thou wolt have no blame,

My banis for to crye   *proclamation; shout*
460 By dayis and bi nighte;
And loke that thou aspye,   *find out*
Ye, bi al thi mighte,

Of Deth and of his maistrye   *power*
Qwher he durst com in sighte,   *Whether he dares*
465 Ogeynis me and my meyné   *Against; retinue*
With force and armis to fighte.

Loke that thou go both est and west
And com ogeyne anone.   *again*
Nuncius Lorde, to wende I am prest,   *go; ready*
470   Lo, now I am gone.

        Et eat pla[team]   *He goes into (or through) the place*

        Pes and listenith to my sawe,   *my words*
        Bothe yonge and olde;
        As ye wol noght ben aslawe   *If you would; slain*
        Be ye neuer so bolde.

475   I am a messager isente
        From the Kyng of Life;
        That ye schal fulfil his talente   *desire*
        On peyne of lym and lif.

        His hestis to hold and his lawe   *orders; uphold*
480   Uche a man on honde;   *Each; here*
        Lest ye be henge and todraw,   *hanged and disembowelled*
        Or kast in hard bonde.   *bondage*

        Ye wittin wel that he is king   *know*
        And lord of al londis,
485   Kepere and maister of al thing
        Within se and sondis.   *From coast to coast*

        I am sente for to enquer   *ask*
        Oboute ferre and nere,
        Yif any man dar werre arere   *If; dare raise war*
490   Agein suche a bachelere.   *young man*

        To wrother hele he was ibore   *misfortune*
        That wold with hym stryve;
        Be him sikir he is ilore   *certain; lost*
        As here in this lyve,

495   Thegh hit wer the King of Deth   *Although*
        And he so hardy were;
        Bot he ne hath might ne meth   *power nor ability*
        The King of Lif to afere;   *frighten*

        Be he so hardy or so wode   *insane*
500   In his londe to aryve,   *arrive*

He wol se his herte-blode   *see his own life-blood*
And he with hym stryve.   *If*

If . . .

 NOTES TO THE PRIDE OF LIFE

ABBREVIATIONS: *CT*: Chaucer, *Canterbury Tales*; *MED*: *Middle English Dictionary*; *OED*: *Oxford English Dictionary*; **s.d.**: stage direction; **Whiting**: Whiting, *Proverbs, Sentences, and Proverbial Phrases*.

4	Although the fragmentary manuscript of the play survived to modern times among the archives of the Augustinian priory of the Holy Trinity, the fact that the playwright invites both the "lered" and the "lewed" to enjoy the play would argue strongly in favor of a public performance, rather than a cloistered audience. Alan J. Fletcher has shown that the priory was involved in other modes of public performance as well (*Drama, Performance, and Polity*, p. 84).
10	The reference to the weather would seem to imply an outdoor performance.
15–112	It is common for medieval drama to present a summary of a play (or cycle), called the banns, before the action begins. The banns were often used as an advertisement, not unlike a modern movie trailer, to generate interest in the play and to announce the performance. Banns were also shouted to spread official news, as in line 459 ("My banis for to crye"). See Introduction, p. 3, and note to line 503.
60	*a wommanis tal*. Coldeway's gloss, "an old wive's tale," has merit, providing an early example of that idiom. *OED* cites Marlowe's *Faust* V.133 as the earliest instance of the gendered saying.
69	*couthe*. I have followed Norman Davis' gloss here ("could"), though Coldeway's "knew" works well too, especially given the sense of *chout* in line 68.
73	*tham*. MS *yam*. Holthausen, following Bradl, reads *ham*. Davis and Coldeway: *than*.
97	The banns do not make it clear if the Virgin Mary's prayers and the king's subsequent redemption actually formed a part of the play, but to make sense of the argument it would seem that they must have done so.
98	There are many dialogue poems consisting of a debate between the body and the soul, both in Middle English and in other European vernaculars. It is not clear in the banns whether this description is intended to describe such a debate on stage or simply to indicate that it is the body's pride (line 95) by which the soul is damned (line 96).
98, 100	Holthausen transposes these two lines; Coldeway follows the transposition, the sense of lines 97–100 thus being: "Through the prayers of Our Lady mild / She would repay all goodness; / She will pray to her son so mild, / [That] the soul and

body shall part ways." Davis glosses "dispyte" as "dispute, contend," but "part ways" gets better at the sense, since the next two stanzas present just such a severance as the body learns the pains of death (lines 101–04) while Mary would reclaim the soul from the fiends so that it might abide (lines 105–08).

110   "Place" here likely has the specific sense of the Latin "platea" (see also line 470 s.d.), the neutral space on the ground which must be constantly renegotiated between actors and audience. The line's meaning then would be: "Don't interfere with our playing area."

126   This is the first break between sections of text in the manuscript in which text has been lost; the faulty rhyme scheme shows that at least two lines of the stanza have disappeared between the blocks of text, as well as the following speech heading.

135   *knytis*. MS: *kyntes*.

213   *undir myne eye*. *Rex* evokes courtly conventions whereby all in the king's presence bow to his authority. Death is viewed here as a member of the court and thus stands in awe of the king's purview.

263   The king's messenger is variously called "Mirth" (Pleasure) and "Solas" (Comfort). He is the king's principal servant, while the two soldiers, Strength and Health, represent the king's protection. Mirth represents the king's primary interests in life, pleasure and creature comforts.

285   *Berewik upon Twede*. A town in the far northeast of England, just south of the Scottish border. Mirth will travel great distances in his king's service.

301   Many suggestions have been made for the identity of "Gailispire on the Hill," most of them in England. Fletcher has shown that the reference is very likely to Giltspur, in the northern part of County Wicklow, not far south of Dublin. In the eighteenth century it was known as Gilsper or Gillspur Hill, and the Augustinian canons of Dublin owned land in the area (*Drama, Performance, and Polity*, pp. 84–86).

302   The earldom of Kent reverted to the crown in 1407, and it is possible that this line could imply a date for the play prior to this, when the title was still in private hands; or after, if *Rex Vivus* is the king of England, as he again has Kent to give as a reward.

303   The king asks Strength to draw the cord which pulls a curtain across a space on the stage, likely an inner room or booth. In its simplest form, this would have been the back part of the stage, separated from the front by the curtain and cord to which he refers. It might well have contained a couch or bed on which the king can take his rest (as in line 304).

322, s.d.   There is no indication of what song Mirth might sing, but any popular tavern song of a secular nature would be appropriate, and the decision might well have been left to the actor. Unfortunately, this is exactly the type of song that is least likely to survive, and no appropriate songs from the later fourteenth century have come down to us. See Appendix 2 for a suggestion.

326	This is the second place where a break between two text blocks also seems to indicate a loss of some text. It might be quite a substantial loss here, since Mirth the messenger needs to explain his errand to the bishop.
327–90	The bishop's complaint is derived from a well-known poem usually called "The Abuses of the Age." Two representative versions are printed in Appendix 1.
332	*Streyint.* The bishop's complaint is not likely a reference to the first soldier, also called "Strength" (line 143 s.n.), but to brute force.
343	*Slet.* The manuscript reads "Slot," which could be an error either for "slet," an unusual word meaning "crafty" or "wise" (cognate with modern English "sleight"), or for "sot," which would be an orthographic variant of "soth" ("true").
362	*gret eteit the smal.* Proverbial; see Whiting G 444. Compare F 232 ("great fish eat the small") and D 146 ("mickle feer heve the little").
380	A writ of "supersedeas" suspends a court's proceedings, generally in favor of a participant's involvement in a case in a higher court. The legal terminology reminds all that they have an irrevocable date with death.
390 s.d.	In the missing lines (see note to line 326), the bishop must have returned to the king, who has emerged from behind the curtain (line 303). The sermon is likely for the king as well as the audience.
401–02	*Det is not the man . . . wil spar.* Coldeway glosses: Death is not "the kind of man / Who will spare you anything."
442	*Then artou but a page.* The bishop suggests the king's power is useless against death, that the king is as powerless against death as a page is to the king.
456	*Solas.* There is only one messenger, alternately named Mirth (lines 263 and 279), later called Solas (lines 295, 321, and 456). This is not a second messenger.
502	I have followed Davis and Coldeway in placing a period at the end of this line despite the fact that the manuscript simply breaks off here.
503	The banns give some indication of the rest of the play, though their description of the action is not entirely clear. Mirth delivers his message to Death, who accepts the king's challenge. In the following battle — defined in the banns as a battle between Life and Death — the King of Life is killed, and his soul is seized by devils. The soul prays to the Virgin Mary for deliverance. The banns do not indicate whether the king's soul is a speaking character, nor whether the soul's prayers to Mary are successful (though the action of the rest of the play would suggest that they are). It is also not clear whether Mary herself appears at the end of the play; although the playwright notes that she "will pray to her son" (line 99) and "will reward goodness" (line 100), the banns do not specify that these are actions which take place as part of the play.

WISDOM

Fyrst enteryde Wysdome in a Ryche purpull clothe of golde, wyth a mantyll of the same ermynnyde wythin, havynge about his neke a ryall hood furred wyth Ermyn, upon hys hede a cheveler [wig] wyth browys [eye-brows], a berde of golde of Sypres [Cyprus] Curlyde, a Ryche Imperyall Crown therupon, sett wyth precyus stonys and perlys. In his leyfte honde, a balle of golde wyth a cros theruppon, and in hys Ryght honde a Regall schepter [scepter], thus seyng:

WYDSOM	Yff ye wyll wet the propyrté	*If; know the meaning*
	Ande the resun of my nayme imperyall,	*significance*
	I am clepyde of hem that in erthe be	*called by those*
	Everlastynge Wysdom, to my noble egalle,	*equal to my nobility*
5	Wyche name accordyt best in especyall,	*suits me best*
	And most to me ys convenyent.	*appropriate*
	Allethow eche persone of the Trinyté be wysdom eternall,	*Although; is*
	And all thre on everlastynge wysdome togedyr present,	*in; [are] present*
	Nevertheles, forasmoche as wysdom ys propyrly	
10	Applyede to the Sune be resune,	*Attributed; Son; reason*
	And also yt fallyt to hym specyally	*belongs*
	Bycause of hys hye generacyon,	*birth*
	Therfor the belovyde Sone hathe this sygnyficacyon,	
	Custummaly Wysdom, now Gode, now man,	*Customarily*
15	Spous of the chyrche and very patrone,	*true*
	Wyffe of eche chose soule — thus Wysdom begane.	*chosen*

Here entrethe Anima as a mayde, in a wyght [white] clothe of gold gyedly purfyled [handsomely bordered] with menyver [fur], a mantyll of blake theruppeon, a cheveler [wig] lyke to Wysdom, wyth a ryche chappelet [coronet] lasyde [fastened] behynde [at the back] hangynge down wyth to [two] knottys of golde and syde tasselys, knelynge down to Wysdom, thus seyng:

[ANIMA]	*"Hanc amavi et exquisivi"* —	*[SOUL] Her have I loved and sought* (Wisdom 8:2)
	Fro my yougthe thys have I soute,	*From; sought*
	To have to my spouse most specyally	
20	For a lover of your schappe am I wroute.	*appearance; created*
	Above all hele and bewty that ever was sought,	*health*
	I have lovyde Wysdom as for my lyght,	
	For alle goodnes wyth hym ys broughte.	
	In wysdom I was made all bewty bryghte!	

25   Of your name the hye felycyté
            No creature knowyt full exposycyon.   *has full understanding*
WYSDAM *"Sapiencia specialior est sole."*[1]
            I am foundon lyghte wythout comparyson,   *created*
            Of sterrys above all the dysposicyon,   *display*
30   Forsothe of lyght the very bryghtnes,   *Truly*
            Meroure of the dyvyne domynacyon,   *Mirror*
                And the image of hys goodnes.

            Wysdom ys better than all worldly precyosnes,
                And all that may dysyryde be
35   Ys not in comparyschon to my lyknes.   *nothing*
                The lengthe of the yerys in my ryght syde be,
                Ande in my lefte syde ryches, joy, and prosperyté.
                    Lo, this ys the worthynes of my name!
ANIMA   A, soveren Wysdom! Yff your benygnyté   *If; kindness*
40   Wolde speke of love, that wer a game!   *pleasure*

WYSDOM Of my love to speke, yt ys myrable.   *wonderful*
            Beholde now, Soull, wyth joyfull mynde,
            How lovely I am, how amyable
                To be halsyde and kyssyde of mankynde.   *embraced*
45   To all clene soulys I am full hende   *ready at hand*
                And ever present wer that they be.   *where*
            I love my lovers wythoutyn ende
                That ther love have stedfast in me.

            The prerogatyff of my love ys so grett
50   That wo tastyt therof the lest droppe sure   *who tastes*
            All lustys and lykyngys worldly shall lett;   *desires; leave*
                They shall seme to hym fylthe and ordure.   *garbage*
                They that of the hevy burthen of synne hathe cure,   *[need of] cure*
                    My love dyschargethe and puryfyethe clene.
55   It strengtheth the mynde, the soull makyt pure,   *strengthens*
                And gevyt wysdom to hem that perfyghte bene.   *gives*
                Wo takyt me to spouse may veryly wene,   *Who; understand*
                    Yff above all thynge ye love me specyally,
                That rest and tranquyllyté he shall sene,   *see*
60   And dey in sekyrnes of joy perpetuall.   *die; certainty*

            The hey worthynes of my love   *high*
                Angell nor man can tell playnly;
            Yt may be felt from experyens above,   *spiritual experience*
                But not spoke ne tolde as yt ys veryly.   *spoken of; truly*

---

[1] *Wisdom is more splendid than the sun* (Wisdom 7:29)

65   The godly love no creature can specyfye.   *describe*
            What wrech is that lovyth not this love,
        That lovyt hys lovers ever so tendyrly,
            That hys syght from them never can remove?

ANIMA   O worthy spouse and soveren father,
70   O swet amyke, our joy, our blys!   *beloved*
        To your love wo dothe repeyer,   *who; turn*
            All felycyté yn that creature ys.
        Wat may I geve you ageyn for this,
            O Creator, lover of your creature?
75   Though be our freelté we do amys,   *because of our frailty*
            Your grett mercy ever sparyth reddure.   *punishment*

        A, soveren Wysdom, *sanctus sanctorum!*   *holy of holies*
            Wat may I geve to your most plesaunce?   *What; greatest pleasure*
WYSDOM "*Fili, prebe michi cor tuum!*"   *Son, give me your heart* (Proverbs 23:26)
80   I aske not ellys of all thi substance;
        Thy clene hert, thi meke obeysance,   *obedience*
            Geve me that and I am contente.   *Give*
ANIMA   A, soveren joy, my hertys affyance!   *greatest*
            The fervoure of my love to you I present,   *display*

85   That mekyt my herte, your love so fervent.   *makes meek*
            Teche me the scolys of your dyvynyté.   *doctrines*
WYSDOM Dysyer not to savour in cunnynge to excellent,   *too complex*
            But drede and conforme your wyll to me,
        For yt ys the heelfull dyscyplyne that in wysdam may be,   *healthy*
90   The drede of God, that ys begynnynge —
        The wedys of synne yt makyt to flee,   *weeds; causes*
            And swete vertuus herbys in the soull sprynge.   *grow*

ANIMA   O endles Wysdom, how may I have knowynge
            Of thi Godhede incomprehensyble?
WYSDOM By knowynge of yoursylff ye may have felynge   *some sense*
96   Wat Gode ys in your soule sensyble.   *[Of] what*
        The more knowynge of your selff passyble,   *[which is] possible*
            The more veryly ye shall God knowe.   *truly*
ANIMA   O soveren Auctoure most credyble,   *Creator*
100   Your lessun I attende as I owe,   *ought*

        I that represent here the soull of man.
            Wat ys a soull, wyll ye declare?
WYSDOM Yt ys the ymage of Gode that all began,
            And not only ymage, but hys lyknes ye are.
105   Of all creaturys the fayrest ye ware   *were*
            Into the tyme of Adamys offence.   *Until*

ANIMA   Lord, sythe we, thy soulys, yet nowt wer ther,   *since*
              Wy of the fyrst man bye we the vyolence?   *Why; pay for*

WYSDOM   For every creature that hath ben or shall
110   Was in natur of the fyrst man, Adame,
              Of hym takynge the fylthe of synne orygynall,
                 For of hym all creaturys cam.
                 Than by hym of reson ye have blame,   *Then because of him reasonably*
                    And be made the brondys of helle.   *firebrands*
115   Wen ye be bore fyrst of your dame,   *When; born; mother*
              Ye may in no wyse in hevyn dwell,

              For ye be dysvyguryde be hys synne,   *disfigured by*
                 Ande dammyde to derknes from Godys syghte.
ANIMA   How dothe grace than ageyn begynne?
120   Wat reformythe the soull to hys fyrste lyght?
WYSDOM   Wysdam, that was Gode and man ryght,
              Made a fulle sethe to the Fadyr of hevyn   *atonement*
              By the dredfull dethe to hym was dyght,   *[which] was ordained*
                 Of wyche dethe spronge the sacramentys sevyn,

125   Wyche sacramentys all synne wasche awey.
              Fyrst baptem clensythe synne orygynall,   *baptism*
          And reformyt the soull in feythe verray   *true*
                 To the gloryus lyknes of Gode eternall
                 Ande makyt yt as fayer and as celestyall
130   As yt never dyffoulyde had be,   *defiled; been*
              Ande ys Crystys own specyall,   *intimate*
                 Hys restynge place, hys plesant see.   *seat*

ANIMA   In a soule watt thyngys be,
              By wyche he hathe his very knowynge?   *true knowledge*
WYSDOM   Tweyn partyes. The on, sensualyté,   *Two parts; sense*
136   Wyche ys clepyde the flechly felynge.   *called; fleshly*
              The fyve outewarde wyttys to hym be servynge;   *senses*
                 Wan they be not reulyde ordynatly,   *ruled properly*
              The sensualyté than, wythoute lesynge,   *falsehood*
140   Ys made the ymage of synne then of his foly.   *because of*

          The other parte, that ys clepyde resone,
              Ande that ys the ymage of Gode propyrly,
          For by that the soull of Gode hath cognycyon,   *knowledge*
              And be that hym servyt and lovevyt duly.   *because of that; loves*
145   Be the neyther parte of reson he knowyt dyscretly   *By; lower; individually*
              All erthely thyngys, how they shall be usyde,   *ought to be*
              What suffysyth to hys myghtys bodely,   *bodily needs*
                 Ande wat nedyt not to be refusyde.

	Thes tweyn do signyfye	
150	Your dysgysynge and your aray,	*costume*
	Blake and wyght, foull and fayer, vereyly,	*white; truly*
	Every soull here — this ys no nay;	*undeniable*
	Blake, by sterynge of synne that cummyth all day,	*stirring*
	Wyche felynge cummythe of sensualyté,	
155	And wyght, be knowenge of reson veray	*true*
	Of the blyssyede infenyt Deyté.	*infinite*

	Thus a soule ys both foulle and fayer:	
	Foull as a best, be felynge of synne,	*beast*
	Fayer as angell, of hevyn the ayer,	*heir*
160	By knowynge of Gode by hys reson wythin.	
ANIMA	Than may I sey thus and begynne	
	With fyve prudent vyrgyns of my reme —	*realm*
	Thow be the fyve wyttys of my soull wythinne —	*Those; senses*
	"Nigra sum sed formosa, filia Jerusalem."[1]	

Her enteryd fyve vyrgynes wyth kertyllys [overskirts] and mantelys wyth chevelers [wigs] and chapelettys [coronets], and syng: "Nigra sum sed formosa, filia Jerusalem, sicut tabernacula cedar et sicut pelles Salomonis."[2]

ANIMA	The doughters of Jerusalem me not lak,	*[find] no flaw in me*
166	For this dyrke schadow I bere of humanyté	*Because of; dark*
	That, as the tabernacull of Cedar wythout, yt ys blake,	
	Ande wythine as the skyn of Salamone, full of bewty.	
	"Quod fusca sum, nolite considerare me,	
170	*Quia decoloravit me sol Jovis."*[3]	
WISDOM	Thus all the soulys that in this lyff be	
	Stondynge in grace, be lyke to thys.	

	A, *quinque prudentes* — your wyttys fyve —	*five prudent ones*
	Kepe you clene, and ye shall never deface,	*be disfigured*
175	Ye Goddys ymage never shall ryve,	*tear apart*
	For the clene soull ys Godys restynge place.	
	Thre myghtys every Cresten soull has,	*powers*
	Wyche bethe applyede to the Trinyté.	*are associated with*
MYNDE	All thre here, lo, byfor your face:	
180	Mynde,	
WYLL	Wyll,	

---

[1] *I am black, but beautiful O ye daughters of Jerusalem* (Canticles 1:4)

[2] *"Nigra . . . Salomonis": I am black, but beautiful, O ye daughters of Jerusalem, as the tents of Cedar, as the curtains of Solomon* (Canticles 1:4)

[3] Lines 169–70: *Because I am dark, look not upon me, / For the sun of Jove has discolored me* (Compare Canticles 1:5)

UNDYRSTONDYNGE   And Undyrstondynge, we thre!

WYSDAM Ye thre declare than thys,
         Your sygnyfycacyon and your propyrté.   *meaning; nature*
MENDE I am Mynde, that in the soule ys
         The veray fygure of the Deyté.   *true*
185   Wen in myselff I have mynde and se   *When*
            The benefyttys of Gode and hys worthynes,
         How holl I was mayde, how fayere, how fre,   *whole; noble*
            How gloryus, how jentyll to hys lyknes,

         Thys insyght bryngyt to my mynde
190   Wat grates I ough to God ageyn,   *What gratitude I owe*
         That thus hathe ordenyde wythout ende
            Me in hys blys ever for to regne.   *reign*
         Than myn insuffycyens ys to me peyn,   *inadequacy*
            That I have not werof to yelde my dett,   *nothing; pay my debt*
195   Thynkynge myselff creature most veyne.   *vain*
            Than for sorow my bren I knett.   *brows I knit*

         Wen in my mynde I brynge togedyr   *When*
            The yerys and dayes of my synfullnes,
         The unstabullnes of my mynde hedyr and thedyr,
200   My oreble fallynge and freellnes,   *horrible failure and frailty*
         Myselff ryght nought than I confes;   *[to be] utterly worthless*
            For by myselff I may not ryse
         Wythout specyall grace of Godys goodnes.
            Thus, mynde makyt me myselff to dyspyse.

205   I seke and fynde nowere comforte,
            But only in Gode, my Creature;   *Creator*
         Than onto hym I do resorte   *unto*
            Ande say, "Have mynde of me, my Savour!"   *Be mindful*
         Thus mynde to mynde bryngyth that favoure;
210   Thus, by mynde of me, Gode I kan know.   *by my own mind*
         Goode mynde, of Gode yt ys the fygure,
            Ande thys mynde to have, all Crysten ow.   *ought*

WYLL And I of the soull am the wyll.
         Of the Godhede lyknes and a fygure;
215   Wyth goode wyll no man may spyll,   *be lost*
         Nor wythout goode wyll of blys be sure.
         Wat soule wyll gret mede recure,   *What; obtain a great reward*
            He must grett wyll have in thought or dede,
         Vertuusly sett wyth consyens pure,
220   For in wyll stondyt only mannys dede.   *in will alone stands man's deed*

Wyll for dede oft ys take;   *deed; understood*
   Therfor the wyll must weell be dysposyde.   *be well-disposed [in virtue]*
Than ther begynnyt all grace to wake,
   Yff wyth synne yt be not anosyde.   *harmed*
225 Therfor the wyll must be wele apposyde,   *examined*
    Or that yt to the mevynge geve consent;   *Before; action*
   The lybrary of reson must be unclosyde,
    Ande aftyr hys domys to take entent.   *judgments; advice*

Our wyll in Gode must be only sett,
230 And for Gode to do wylfully;
Wan gode wyll resythe, God ys in us knett,   *When; rises; entwined*
   Ande he performyt the dede veryly.   *truly*
Of hym cummyth all wyll sett perfyghtly,
   For of ourselff we have ryght nought   *nothing at all*
235 But syne, wrechydnes, and foly.   *sin*
    He ys begynner and gronde of wyll and thought.   *basis*

Than this goode wyll seyde before   *mentioned*
   Ys behovefulle to yche creature,   *appropriate to each*
Iff he cast hym to restore   *intends*
240 The soule that he hath take of cure,   *taken into his care*
   Wyche of God ys the fygure,
    As longe as the fygure ys kept fayer,
   Ande ordenyde ever to endure
    In blys, of wyche ys he the veray hayer.   *heir*

UNDYRSTONDYNGE The thyrde parte of the soule ys undyrstondynge.
246 For by understondyng I beholde wat Gode ys   *what*
In hymselff, begynnyng wythout begynnynge,
   Ande ende wythout ende, that shall never mys.   *fail*
   Incomprehensyble in hymselff he ys;
250   Hys werkys in me I kan not comprehende,
   How shulde I holly hym than, that wrought all this?   *worship*
    Thus, by knowynge of me, to knowynge of Gode I assende.   *ascend*

I know in angelys he ys desyderable,   *among; desirable*
   For hym to beholde thei dysyer soverenly;   *above all else*
255 In hys seyntys, most dylectable,
   For in hymm thei joy assyduly;   *assiduously*
In creaturys hys werkys ben most wondyrly,   *wonderful*
   For all ys made by hys myght,
By hys wysdom governyde most soverenly,
260 And his benygnyté inspyryt all soullys wyth lyght.   *kindness*

Of all creaturys he ys lovyde sovereyn,   *beloved*
   For he ys Gode of yche creature,   *each*

	And they be his peple that ever shall reynge,	*reign*
	In wom he dwellyt as his tempull sure.	*whom*
265	Wan I of thys knowynge make reporture,	*When; declaration*
	Ande se the love he hathe for me wrought,	*see*
	Yt bryngyt me to love that Prynce most pure,	
	For, for love, that Lorde made man of nought.	
	Thys ys that love wyche ys clepyde charyté;	
270	For Gode ys charyté, as autors tellys,	*authors*
	Ande woo ys in charyté, in Gode dwellyt he,	*who*
	Ande Gode, that is charyté, in hym dwellys.	
	Thus, undyrstondynge of Gode compellys	*compels [us]*
	To cum to charyté — than have hys lyknes, lo!	
275	Blyssyde ys that soull that this speche spellys:	*utters*
	"*Et qui creavit me requievit in tabernaculo meo.*"[1]	

Wysdom	Lo, thes thre myghtys in on soule be:	*each*
	Mynde, Wyll, and Undyrstondynge.	
	By Mynde, of Gode the Fadyr knowyng have ye;	
280	By Undyrstondynge, of Gode the Sone ye have knowynge;	
	By Wyll, wyche turnyt into love brennynge,	
	Gode the Holy Gost, that clepyde ys Love,	
	Not thre Godys, but on Gode in beynge.	*one*
	Thus eche clene soule ys symylytude of Gode above.	*pure; image*

285	By Mynde, feythe in the Father have we;	
	Hoppe in our Lorde Jhesu by Undyrstondynge;	*Hope*
	Ande be Wyll, in the Holy Gost, charyté.	
	Lo, thes thre pryncypall vertus of you thre sprynge.	
	Thys the clene soule stondyth as a kynge;	*Thus the pure*
290	Ande above all this ye have free wyll.	
	Of that be ware befor all thynge,	*careful*
	For yff that perverte, all this dothe spylle.	*go astray; perish*

	Ye have thre enmyes, of hem beware:	
	The Worlde, the Flesche, and the Fende.	*Devil*
295	Your fyve wyttys from hem ye spare,	*senses; protect*
	That the sensualyté they brynge not to mynde.	
	Nothynge shulde offende Gode in no kynde,	*manner*
	Ande yff ther do, se that the nether parte of resone	*see; lower*
	In no wys therto lende;	*participate*
300	Than the over parte shall have fre domynacyon.	*Then the higher; full control*

---

[1] *And he who created me rested in my tabernacle* (Ecclesiasticus 24:11–12)

Wan suggestyon to the Mynde doth apere,   *When*
  Undyrstondynge, delyght not ye therin!
Consent not, Wyll, yll lessons to lere!   *evil; learn*
  Ande than suche steryngys by no syn;   *impulses be*
305   Thei do but purge the soule wer ys such contraversye.   *where*
      Thus in me, Wysdom, your werkys begynne;
   Fyght, and ye shall have the crown of glory,
      That ys everlastynge joy to be parteners therinne!

ANIMA   Soveren Lorde, I am bounde to thee!
310   Wan I was nought, thou made me thus gloryus,   *When*
   Wan I perysschede thorow synne, thou savyde me,
      Wen I was in grett perell, thou kept me, Cristus,
      Wen I erryde, thou reducyde me, Jhesus,   *wandered; led me back*
        Wen I was ignorant, thou taut me truthe,
315   Wen I synnyde, thou corecte me thus,   *corrected*
        Wen I was hevy, thou comfortede me by ruthe.   *sad; with pity*

   Wan I stonde in grace, thou holdyste me that tyde,
      Wen I fall, thou reysyst me myghtyly,   *lifted me up*
   Wen I go wyll, thou art my gyde,   *go astray*
320   Wen I cum, thou receyvyste me most lovynly.   *lovingly*
      Thou hast anoyntyde me with the oyll of mercy,
        Thy benefyttys, Lorde, be innumerable.
      Werfor, laude endeles to thee I crye,   *praise*
        Recomendynge me to thin endles powre durable.   *everlasting*

Here in the goynge out, the fyve wyttys [senses] synge: "Tota pulcra es, et cetera,"[1] they goyng
befor, Anima next, and her folowynge, Wysdom, and aftyr hym, Mynde, Wyll, and
Undyrstondynge, all thre in wight [white] cloth of golde, cheveleryde [wigged] and crestyde
[crowned] in sute [in the same manner]. And aftyr the songe, entreth Lucyfer in a devellys aray
wythout, and wythin as a prowde galonte [fashionable man], seynge thus on thys wyse:

LUCYFER   Out, harow, I rore!
326   For envy I lore.   *frown (lour)*
   My place to restore,
      God hath made man!
   All cum thei not thore,   *If they do not all come there*
330   Woode and they wore,   *Mad; were*
   I shall tempte hem so sorre,   *them most sorely*
      For I am he that syn begane!

   I was a angell of lyghte,
   Lucyfeer I hyght,   *was called*

---

[1] *You are completely beautiful, etc.* (Canticles 4:7)

335 Presumynge in Goddys syght,
        Werfor I am lowest in hell!
     In reformynge of my place ys dyght   *placed*
     Man, whom I have in most dyspyght,   *hold in greatest contempt*
     Ever castynge me wyth hem for to fyght,   *devoting myself*
340   In that hevynly place he shulde not dwell.   *[So that] in*

     I am as wyly now as than,   *crafty*
     The knowynge that I hade, yet I can;   *knowledge; still*
     I know all compleccyons of man,
        Werto he ys most dysposyde.   *inclined*
345 Ande therin I tempte hym ay-whan;   *whenever*
     I marre hys myndys to ther wan,   *confuse; weakness*
     That whoo ys hym that God hym began!   *woe; created*
        Many a holy man wyth me ys mosyde!   *deceived*

     Of Gode, man ys the fygure,
350 Hys symylytude, hys pyctoure,   *image*
     Gloryosest of ony creature
        That ever was wrought.
     Wyche I wyll dysvygure   *disfigure*
     Be my fals conjecture!   *By; trickery*
355 Yff he tende my reporture,   *If; listens to my speech*
        I shall brynge hym to nought!

     In the Soule ben thre partyes, iwys: *parts, indeed*
     Mynde, Wyll, Undyrstondynge of blys —
     Fygure of the Godhede — I know wele thys!
360   And the flesche of man that ys so changeable,
     That wyll I tempte, as I gees;   *intend*
     Thou that I pervert, synne noon is   *Though; pervert [it], [it] is no sin*
     But yff the Soule consent to mys,   *Unless; sin*
        For in the Wyll of the Soule the dedys ben damnable.   *deeds*

365 To the Mynde of the Soule I shall mak suggestyun,
     Ande brynge hys Undyrstondynge to dylectacyon,   *pleasure*
     So that hys Wyll make confyrmacyon.
        Than am I sekyr inowe   *certain enough*
     That dede shall sew of damnacyon!   *result in*
370 Than of the Soull the Devll hath dominacyon.
     I wyll go make hys examynacyon,
        To all the devllys of helle I make a vowe!

     But, for to tempte man in my lyknes,
     Yt wolde brynge hym to grett feerfullnes!
375 I wyll change me into bryghtnes,
        And so hym to begyle.

Sen I shall schew hym perfyghtnes,
And vertu, prove yt wykkydnes.[1]
Thus undyr colors, all thynge perverse.   *[I will] pervert all things under false pretenses*
380   I shall never rest tyll the Soule I defyle!

    Her Lucyfer devoydyth, and cummyth in ageyn as a goodly galont.   *exits; gallant*

MYNDE   My mynde ys ever on Jhesu
    That enduyde us wyth vertu;   *endowed*
    Hys doctrine to sue   *follow*
      Ever I purpose.   *intend*
UNDYRSTONDYNGE   My undyrstondynge ys in trew,   *the true God*
386   That wyth feyth us dyd renew.
    Hys laws to pursew
      Ys swetter to me than savoure of the rose.

WYLL   And my wyll ys hys wyll, veraly,   *truly*
390   That made us hys creaturys so specyally,
    Yeldynge unto hym laude and glory
      For his goodnes.
LUCYFER   Ye fonnyde fathers, founders of foly,   *foolish*
    Vt quid hic statis tota die ociosi?[2]
395   Ye wyll perysche or ye yt aspye;   *before; notice*
    The Devyll hath acumberyde you expres!   *overwhelmed you surely*

    Mynde, Mynde, ser, have in mynde thys!
MYNDE   He ys not ydyll that wyth Gode ys.
LUCYFER   No, ser, I prove well yis!   *yes*
400   Thys ys my suggestyun:
    All thynge hat dew tymes —   *things have appropriate*
    Prayer, fastynge, labour — all thes;
    Wan tyme ys not kept, that dede is amys.   *When; action is wrong*
      The more pleynerly to your informacyon.   *obviously for*

    [To a member of the audience.]

405   Here ys a man that lyvyt wordly,   *lives worldly*
    Hathe wyffe, chylderne, and servantys besy,   *busy*
    And other chargys that I not specyfye!   *I will not*
      Ys yt leeffull to this man   *lawful*
      To leve hys labour usyde truly?[3]
410   Hys chargys perysche, that Gode gaff duly,   *[To let] his dependents*

---

[1] Lines 377–78: *I shall make it appear to him that perfection is sin, / And prove virtue to be wickedness*

[2] *Why do you stand the whole day here in idleness?* (Matthew 20:6)

[3] *To abandon the job that properly belongs to him*

Ande geve hym to preyer and es of body? *comfort*
Woso do thus, wyth God ys not than! *Whoever does*

Mertha plesyde Gode grettly thore. *there*
MYNDE   Ye, but Maria plesyde hymm moche more!
LUCYFER   Yet the lest hade blys for evermore — *lesser*
416   Ys not this anow? *enough*
MYNDE   Contemplatyff lyff ys sett befor. *higher*
LUCYFER   I may not beleve that in my lore, *learning*
For God hymselff, wan he was man borre, *when; born as man*
420   Wat lyff lede he? Answer thou now!

Was he ever in contemplacyon?
MYNDE   I suppos not, be my relacyon. *by what I can say*
LUCYFER   And all hys lyff was informacyon *instruction*
Ande example to man!
425   Sumtyme wyth synners he had conversacyon,
Sumtyme with holy also comunycacyon, *holy [men]*
Sumtyme he laboryde, preyde; sumtyme tribulacyon.
Thys was *vita mixta*, that Gode here began, *the mixed life*

And that lyff shulde ye here sewe. *follow*
MYNDE   I kan not beleve thys ys trewe.
LUCYFER   Contemplatyff lyff for to sewe, *follow*
432   Yt ys grett drede, and se cause why: *very difficult; see the reason*
They must fast, wake, and prey ever new, *continually*
Use harde lyvynge, and goynge wyth dyscyplyne dew, *appropriate*
435   Kepe sylence, wepe, and surphettys eschewe; *excess*
Ande yff they fayll of thys, they offende Gode hyghly.

Wan they have wastyde be feyntnes,
Than febyll ther wyttys and fallyn to fondnes, *[become] feeble; foolishness*
Sum into dyspeyer and sum into madnes. *despair*
440   Wet yt well, God ys not plesyde wyth thys! *Know*
Leve, leve such syngler besynes! *curious behavior*
Be in the worlde! Use thyngys nesesse! *necessary*
The comyn ys best expres. *ordinary; certainly*
444   Who clymyt hye, hys fall gret ys! *climbs*

MYNDE   Truly, me seme ye have reson. *it seems to me*
LUCYFER   Aplye you then to this conclusyun. *Consider*
MYNDE   I kan make no replicacyon, *reply*
Your resons be grete!
I kan not forgett this informacyon.
LUCYFER   Thynke theruppon, yt ys your salvacyon!
451   Now, and Undyrstondynge wolde have delectacyon, *if; pleasure*
All syngler devocyons he wolde lett. *special; leave*

Your fyve wyttys abrode lett sprede!   *senses*
Se how comly to man ys precyus wede;   *fine clothing*
455   Wat worschype yt ys to be manfull in dede.   *What honor*
        That bryngyt in dominacyon!   *leads to*
Of the symple, what profyght yt to tak hede?   *to pay attention*
Beholde how ryches dystroyt nede!
It makyt man fayer, hym wele for to fede   *himself; feed*
460   And of lust and lykynge commyth generacyon!   *from desire; pleasure; procreation*

Undyrstondynge, tender ye this informacyon?   *value*
UNDYRSTONDYNGE   In thys I fele in manere of dylectacyon!   *a sort of pleasure*
LUCYFER   A ha, ser! Then ther make a pawsacyon!   *pause*
        Se and beholde the worlde aboute!
465   Lytyll thynge suffysyt to salvacyon.
All maner synnys dystroyt contryscyon,   *All kinds of; contrition*
They that dyspeyer mercy have grett compunccyon!   *anxiety*
        Gode plesyde best wyth goode wyll, no dowte!   *is pleased*

Therfor, Wyll, I rede you inclyne.   *advise you to listen*
470   Leve your stodyes, thow ben dyvyn —   *studies, those that are*
Your prayers, your penance, of ipocryttys the syne —   *hypocrites the sign*
        Ande lede a comun lyff!
What synne ys in met? In ale? In wyn?   *food*
Wat synne ys in ryches? In clothynge fyne?
475   All thynge Gode ordenyde to man to inclyne.   *accept*
        Leve your nyse chastyté, and take a wyff!   *foolish*

Better ys fayer frut than foull pollucyon!   *fruit*
What seyth sensualité to this conclusyon?
WYLL   As the fyve wyttys gyff informacyon,   *senses*
480   Yt semyth your resons be goode.
LUCYFER   The Wyll of the Soule hathe fre dominacyon,
Dyspute not to moche in this wyth reson,
Yet the nethyr parte to this taketh sum instruccyon,   *lower*
        And so shulde the over parte, but he were woode.   *higher; unless; insane*

WYLL   Me seme, as ye sey, in body and soule,   *It seems to me*
486   Man may be in the worlde, and be ryght goode.
LUCYFER   Ya, ser, by Sent Powle!   *St. Paul*
        But trust not thes prechors, for they be not goode,
        For they flatere and lye as they wore wood —   *were mad*
490   Ther ys a wolffe in a lombys skyn!   *lamb's*
WYLL   Ya, I woll no more row ageyn the floode.   *against*
        I woll sett my soule on a mery pynne!   *mood*

LUCYFER   Be my trouthe, than do ye wyslye!
        Gode lovyt a clene soull and a mery!   *loves*

495   Acorde you thre togedyr by,   *Agree*
    And ye may not mysfare.
Mynde   To this suggestyon agre we!
Undyrstondynge   Delyght therin I have truly!
Wyll   And I consent therto frelye!
Lucyfer   A, ser! All mery than, awey care!

501   Go in the worlde, se that aboute!   *look around*
    Geet goode frely, cast no doute!   *goods*
    To the ryche ye se men lowly lought!   *see; bow down low*
    Geve to your body that ys nede,   *necessary*
505   Ande ever be mery! Let revell route!   *run riot*
Mynde   Ya, ellys I beschrew my snoute!   *curse*
Undyrstondynge   And yff I care, cache I the goute!   *may I catch*
Wyll   And yff I spare, the Devyll me spede!

Lucyfer   Go your wey than, and do wysly.
510   Change that syde aray!   *long garment*
Mynde   I yt defye!
Undyrstondynge   We woll be fresche, and it hap *La plu joly!*   *The most beautiful*
    Farwell, penance!
Mynde   To worschyppys I wyll my mynde aplye!   *riches*
Undyrstondynge   Myn undyrstondynge in worschyppys and glory!   *riches*
Wylle   And I in lustys of lechery,
515   As was sumtyme gyse of Fraunce!   *custom*
      Wyth "Wy, wyppe!   *Why, quickly*
      Farwell," quod I, "the Devyll ys uppe!"

    Exient.   *They leave*

Lucyfer   Of my dysyere now have I summe!
    Wer onys brought into custume,   *Were it once; habit*
520   Then farwell, consyens, he wer clumme   *[if] he were silent*
    I shulde have all my wyll!
    Resone I have made both deff and dumme,
    Grace ys out and put arome,   *at a distance*
    Wethyr I wyll have, he shall cum,   *Wherever I want him*
525   So, at the last, I shall hym spyll!   *destroy*

    I shall now stere his mynde   *direct*
    To that syne made me a fende,
    Pryde, wyche ys ageyn kynde,   *against nature*
    And of synnys hede.   *chief*
530   So to covetyse he shall wende,   *turn*
    For that enduryth to the last ende,
    And onto lechery, and I may hymm rende!   *if I may lead him*
    Than am I seker the Soule ys dede!   *certain*

That Soule Gode made incomparable,

535   To hys lyknes most amyable,

I shall make yt most reprovable,   *reprehensible*

    Evyn lyke to a fende of hell.

At hys deth I shall apere informable,   *with information*

Schewynge hym all hys synnys abhomynable,

540   Prevynge his Soule dampnable,   *Proving*

    So wyth dyspeyer I shall hym quell.   *destroy*

Wyll clennes ys in mankyn,   *While innocence*

Verely, the Soule God ys wythin,   *Truly*

Ande wen yt ys in dedly synne,   *when*

545   Yt ys veryly the Develys place.   *truly*

Thus by colours and false gynne,   *deceit; strategy*

Many a soule to hell I wynn;

Wyde to go, I may not blyne,   *Far; cease*

    Wyth this fals boy — God gyff hym evell grace!

Her he takyt a schrewede boy wyth hym and goth hys wey, cryenge.   *mischievous*

Mynde Lo, me here in a newe aray!   *garment*

551   Wyppe, wyrre, care awey!   *Quick, hurry*

    Farwell, perfeccyon!

Me semyt myselff most lykly, ay!   *handsome, yes*

It ys but honest, no pryde, no nay.   *the truth; denying*

555   I wyll be freshest by my fay,   *faith*

    For that acordyt wyth my complexccyon.   *suits; temperament*

Undyrstondynge Ande have here me as fresche as you!   *here is*

All mery, mery and glade now!

I have get goode, God wott how!   *goods; knows*

560   For joy I sprynge, I sckyppe!

Goode makyt on mery, to God a vowe!   *Goods; one*

Farewell, consyens, I know not you!

I am at eas, hade I inowe.   *would be; if I had enough*

    Truthe on syde I lett hym slyppe.   *let it slip aside*

Wyll Lo, here on as jolye as ye!   *one*

566   I am so lykynge, me seme I fle!   *happy, it seems to me I fly*

I have atastyde lust! Farwell, chastité!   *tasted*

    My hert ys evermore lyght!

I am full of felycyté!

570   My delyght ys all in bewté.

Ther ys no joy but that in me.

    A woman me semyth a hevynly syght!   *seems to me*

MYNDE   Ande thes ben my synglere solace: *particular pleasures*
        Kynde, fortune, and grace.   *Nature*
575   Kynde, nobley of kynrede me gevyn hase,   *nobility of kindred*
        Ande that makyt me soleyn.   *haughty*
        Fortune in worldys worschyppe me doth lace;   *wrap*
        Grace gevyt curryus eloquens, and that mase   *subtle; causes*
            That alle oncunnynge I dysdeyn!   *ignorance*

UNDYRSTONDYNGE   And my joy ys especyall
581   To hurde uppe ryches for fer to fall,   *hoard; fear of a*
        To se yt, to handyll it, to tell yt all —   *count*
            And streightly to spare!   *frugally; save*
        To be holde ryche and reyall   *considered*
585   I bost, I avaunt wer I shall.   *brag wherever I want*
        Ryches makyt a man equall
            To hem sumtyme hys sovereyngys were.   *those who once were his superiors*

WYLL   To me ys joy most laudable
        Fresche dysgysynge to seme amyable,   *clothing; friendly*
590   Spekynge wordys delectable
            Perteynynge onto love!
        It ys joy of joys inestymable
        To halse, to kys the affyable!   *embrace; lover*
        A lover ys son perceyvable   *soon apparent*
595   Be the smylynge on me wan yt doth remove!   *when it arouses passion*

MYNDE   To avaunte thus, me semeth no schame,   *boast; it seems to me*
        For galontys now be in most fame.   *gallants*
        Curtely personys men hem proclame.   *Courtly*
            Moche we be sett bye!   *We are highly regarded*
UNDYRSTONDYNGE   The ryche covetouse, wo dare blame   *who*
601   Off govell and symony thow he bere the name?   *usury; accusation*
        To be fals, men report yt game!   *call it sport*
            Yt ys clepyde wysdom! "Ware that," quod Ser Wyly!   *called; Beware of; Wily*

WYLL   Ande of lechory to make avaunte,
605   Men fors it no more than drynke ataunt.   *consider; in excess*
        Thes thyngys be now so conversant,   *common*
            We seme yt no schame.   *We consider it*
MYNDE   Curyous aray I wyll ever hante!   *Elaborate clothing; use*
UNDYRSTONDYNGE   Ande I falsnes, to be passante!   *stylish*
WYLL   Ande I in lust my flesche to daunte!   *satisfy*
611   No man dyspyes thes — they be but game!   *despises; sport*

MYNDE   I rejoys of thes, now let us synge!
UNDYRSTONDYNGE   Ande yff I spar, evell joy me wrynge!   *refrain; hurt*

WYLL   Have at, quod I! Lo, howe I sprynge!   *Go on; dance*
615   Lust makyth me wondyr wylde!   *wonderfully*
MYNDE   A tenour to you bothe I brynge.
UNDYRSTONDYNGE   And I a mene for ony kynge!   *middle part [good enough] for*
WYLL   And but a trebull I outwrynge,   *unless an upper part I squeeze out*
619   The Devell hym spede that myrth exyled!

        Et cantent.   *And they sing*

MYNDE   How be this trow ye nowe?   *think*
UNDYRSTONDYNGE   At the best, to God a vowe!   *Terrific*
WYLL   As mery as the byrde on bow,   *bough*
623   I take no thought!   *I haven't a care*
MYNDE   The welfare of this worlde ys in us, I avowe!
UNDYRSTONDYNGE   Lett eche man tell hys condycyons howe.   *reasons*
WYLL   Begynne ye, ande have at yow!   *Go ahead*
        For I am aschamyde of ryght nought.   *nothing at all*

MYNDE   Thys ys a cause of my worschyppe: *the reason for*
        I serve myghty lordeschyppe,
630   Ande am in grett tenderschyppe;   *stewardship*
          Therfor moche folke me dredys.   *many people fear me*
        Men sew to my frendeschyppe   *seek*
        For meyntnance of her shendeschyppe.   *support; shameful behavior*
        I support hem by lordeschyppe
635   For, to get good, this a grett spede ys!   *goods; very successful*

UNDYRSTONDYNGE   And I use joroury,   *bear false witness*
        Enbrace questys of perjury,   *jury of inquiry*
        Choppe and chonge with symonye,   *Bargain and trade*
          And take large geftys!   *bribes*
640   Be the cause never so try,   *certain*
        I preve yt fals — I swere, I lye! —
        Wyth a quest of myn affye.   *jury I have bought*
          The redy wey this now to thryfte ys!   *prosperity*

WYLL   And wat trow ye be me?   *what do you think of*
645   More than I take, spende I threys thre!
          Sumtyme I geff, sumtyme they me,   *[give] to me*
          Ande am ever fresche and gay!
        Few placys now ther be
        But onclennes we shall ther see.   *lechery*
650   It ys holde but a nysyté,   *trivial thing*
          Lust ys now cumun as the way!   *common*

Mynde   Law procedyth not for meyntnance.   *because of bribery*
Undyrstondynge   Trouthe recurythe not for habundance.[1]
Wyll   And lust ys in so grett usance,   *usage*
655   We fors yt nought.   *regard*
Mynde   In us the worlde hath most affyance.   *reliance*
Undyrstondynge   Non thre be in so grett aqueynttance.   *so well known*
Wyll   Few ther be outhe of our allyance;   *out*
659   Wyll the worlde ys thus, take we no thought!   *While; we have no care*

Mynde   Thought? Nay, therageyn stryve I!   *against that*
Undyrstondynge   We have that nedyt us, so thryve I!   *what we need*
Wyll   And yff that I care, never wyve I!   *I'll never marry*
663   Lett hem care that hathe for to sewe!   *who need to sue*
Mynde   Wo lordschyppe shall sew must yt bye!   *Who; sue; pay for*
Undyrstondynge   Wo wyll have law must have monye!   *Who*
Wyll   Ther povert ys the malewrye,   *poverty; misfortune*
           Thow right be, he shall never renewe.   *Though his cause be right; recover*

Mynde   Wronge ys born upe boldly,   *supported*
           Thow all the worlde know yt opynly;
670   Mayntnance ys now so myghty,   *Unjust Support*
           Ande all is for mede!   *bribery*
Undyrstondynge   The lawe ys so coloryde falsly   *perverted*
           By sleyttys and by perjury,   *tricks*
           Brybys be so gredy,
675   That to the pore trouth is take ryght non hede!

Wyll   Wo gett or loose, ye be ay wynnande!   *Who; always winning*
           Mayntnance and perjury now stande: *Unjust Support*
           Thei wer never so moche reynande   *in control*
           Seth Gode was bore!   *Since; born*
Mynde   Ande lechery was never more usande   *being practiced*
681   Of lernyde and lewyde in this lande!   *By; uneducated*
Undyrstondynge   So we thre be now in hande!   *agreement*
Wyll   Ya, and most usyde everywere!

Mynde   Now wyll we thre do make a dance
685   Of thow that longe to our retenance,   *those; belong; retinues*
           Cummynge in by contenance,   *with masks*
           This were a dysporte!
Undyrstondynge   Therto I geve acordance
           Of thow that ben of myn affyance.   *those; company*
Wyll   Let se betyme, ye, Meyntnance!   *Let's see immediately*
691   Clepe in fyrst your resorte!   *Call; retinue*

---

[1] *Truth does not collect damage because of wealth*

Here entur six dysgysed in the sute [livery] of Mynde, wyth rede berdys, and lyouns rampaunt on here crestys [badges], and yche a warder [staff] in hys honde; her [their] mynstrallys, trumpes [trumpets]. Eche answere for hys name.

MYNDE Let se, cum in Indignacyon and Sturdynes! *Stubbornness*
Males also, and Hastynes! *Malice; Rashness*
Wreche and Dyscorde expres! *Vengeance; for certain*
695 And the sevente am I, Mayntennance! *Unjust Support*
Seven ys a numbyr of discorde and inperfyghtnes; *imperfection*
Lo, here ys a yomandrye wyth loveday to dres! *yeomanry to decorate (dress) a loveday*
Ande the Devle hade swore yt, they wolde ber up falsnes, *If; commanded*
Ande maynten yt at the best. This ys the Devllys dance!

700 Ande here menstrellys be convenyent, *appropriate*
For trumpys shulde blow to the jugemente! *trumpets; at a*
Off batell also yt ys on instrumente, *an*
Gevynge comfort to fyght. *in a fight*
Therfor they be expedyente *useful*
705 To thes meny of Mayntement. *this retinue of Unjust Support*
Blow! Lett see Madam Regent,
Ande daunce, ye laddys, your hertys be lyght!

[They dance.]

Lo, that other spare, thes meny wyll spende! *that which others save, this retinue*
UNDYRSTONDYNGE Ya, wo ys hym shall hem offende! *woe*
WYLL Wo wyll not to hem condescende, *Who*
711 He shall have threttys! *threats*
MYNDE They spyll that law wolde amende! *destroy those whom*
UNDYRSTONDYNGE Yit Mayntnance no man dare reprehende.
WYLL Thes meny thre synnys comprehende: *This retinue; comprises*
715 Pryde, Invy, and Wrathe in hys hestys! *Envy; demands*

UNDYRSTONDYNGE Now wyll I than begyn my traces. *my dance*
Jorour in on hoode beer to facys: *one; bears two*
Fayer speche and falsehede in on space ys! *one*
Is it not ruthe? *a pity*
720 The quest of Holborn cum into this placys, *inquest (jury)*
Ageyn the ryght ever ther rechase ys; *Against; judicial review*
Of wom they holde not, harde hys grace ys. *Whomever they rule against*
Many a tyme have dammyde truthe. *they have condemned*

Here entrethe six jorours in a sute [matching livery], gownyde, wyth hodys [hoods] about her nekys, hattys of Meyntenance therupon, vyseryde [masked] diversly; here [their] mynstrell, a bagpype.

UNDYRSTONDYNGE Let se, fyrst Wronge and Sleyght!

725   Dobullnes and Falsnes, schew your myght!   *Duplicity*
       Now Raveyn and Dyscheyit!   *Plunder and Deceit*
          Now holde you here togydyr!
       This menys consyens ys so streytt   *retinue's; limited*
       That they report as mede yevyt beyght!   *they report being bought as earnings*
730   Here ys the quest of Holborn, an evyll endyrecte.   *a crooked (dishonest) evil*
       They daunce all the londe, hydyr and thedyr!
          And I, Perjury, your founder!
          Now dance on, us all! The worlde doth on us wondyr!   *all of us*

[*They dance.*]

734   Lo, here ys a meyné love wellfare!   *retinue [that] loves*
MYNDE Ye, they spende that tru men spare!   *that which; save*
WYLL Have they a brybe, have they no care
          Wo hath wronge or ryght!   *Who*
MYNDE They fors not to swere and starre.   *think nothing of*
WYLL Though all be false, les and mare.
UNDYRSTONDYNGE Wyche wey to the woode wyll the hare?
741   They knewe, and they at rest sett als tyghte!   *know; sit tight [and wait]*
          Some seme hem wyse   *seem to them*
          For the fadyr of us, Covetyse.   *Covetousness*

WYLL Now Meyntnance and Perjury   *Unjust Support*
745   Hathe schewyde the trace of ther cumpeny,   *dance*
       Ye shall se a sprynge of Lechery,   *dance*
          That to me attende!
       Here forme ys of the stewys clene rebaldry!   *Their; brothel's pure*
       They wene sey soth wen that they lye!   *think they tell the truth*
750   Of the comyn they synge, eche wyke by and by!   *Regularly; each week continually*
          They may sey wyth tenker, I trow, 'Lat amende!'   *tinker; Get it fixed*

Here entreth six women in sut [matching liveries], thre dysgysyde as galontes [gallants] and thre as matrones, wyth wondyrfull vysurs [masks] conregent [similar]; here [their] mynstrell, an hornepype.

WYLL Cum slepers, Rekleshede and Idyllnes,   *Carelessness*
          All in, all — Surfet and Gredynes,   *Every one in*
          For the flesche, Spousebreche and Mastres,   *Adultery; Mistress*
755   Wyth jentyll Fornycacyon.
          Your mynstrell a hornepype mete   *appropriate*
          That foull ys in hymselff but to the erys swete.   *ears*
          Thre fortherers of love: "Hem shrew I!" quod Bete.   *I curse him*
759   Thys dance of this damesellys ys thorow this regyn.   *these; region*

[*They dance.*]

MYNDE   Ye may not endure wythout my meyntenance.   *support*
UNDYRSTONDYNGE   That ys bought wyth a brybe of our substance.
WYLL   Whow, breydest thou us of thin aqueyntance?   *Whoa, reproach*
       I sett thee at nought!
MYNDE   On that worde I woll tak vengeaunce!
765   Wer vycys be gederyde, ever ys sum myschance.   *Where; assembled*
       Hurle hens thes harlottys! Here gyse ys of France.   *Throw out; Their manner*
       They shall abey bytterly, by hym that all wrought!   *suffer*

UNDYRSTONDYNGE   Ill spede thee ande thou spare!   *if you delay*
       Thi longe body bare
770   To bett I not spare.   *To beat I will*
       Have thee ageyn!   *Have at*
WYLL   Holde me not! Let me go! Ware!   *Beware*
       I dynge, I dasche! Ther, go ther!   *beat; strike*
       Dompe devys, can ye not dare?   *Dumb show; shut up*
775   I tell yow, outwarde, on and tweyn!   *forward, one and two*

       Exient.   *They [the dancers] leave*

MYNDE   Now I schrew yow thus dansaunde!   *curse; dancing*
UNDERSTONDYNGE   Ye, and evyll be thou thryvande!   *may you thrive evilly*
WYLL   No more let us be stryvande.   *fighting*
779   Nowe all at on!   *as one*
MYNDE   Here was a meny onthryvande!   *a useless retinue*
UNDYRSTONDYNGE   To the Devll be they dryvande.   *going*
WYLL   He that ys yll wyvande,   *badly married*
       Wo hys hym, by the bon!   *Woe is; bone*

MYNDE   Leve then this dalyance   *playing*
785   Ande set we a ordenance   *plot*
       Off better chevesaunce   *profit*
       How we may thryve.
UNDYRSTONDYNGE   At Westmyster, wythout varyance,   *Westminster; question*
       The nex terme shall me sore avaunce,   *next [law] period; greatly advance*
790   For retornys, for enbraces, for recordaunce.   *writ payments; bribery; false testimony*
       Lyghtlyer to get goode kan no man on lyve!   *More easily; goods*

MYNDE   Ande at the parvyse I wyll be   *church door*
       A Powlys betwyn to ande thre,   *At St. Paul's; two*
       Wyth a menye folowynge me,   *retinue*
795   Entret, juge-partynge, and to-supporte.   *jury-bribery (judge-bribery); illegal support*
WYLL   Ande ever the latter, the lever me.   *the better for*
       Wen I com lat to the cyté   *When; late [at night]*
       I walke all lanys and weys to myn affynyté.   *street; with my companions*
799   And I spede no ther, to the stews I resort.   *If I succeed not; brothels*

MYNDE	Ther gettys thou nouhte, but spendys.	*nothing*
WYLL	Yis, sumtyme I take amendys	*fines*
	Of hem that nought offendys,	*have done nothing wrong*
	I engrose upe here purs.	*take possession of*
MYNDE	And I arest ther no drede ys,	*fear*
805	Preve forfett ther no mede ys,	*Take forfeit; reward*
	Ande take to me that nede ys.	*necessary*
	I reke not thow they curs.	*care not though*

UNDYRSTONDYNGE	Thow they curs, nether the wers I fare.	*Though*
	Thys day I endyght them I herde of never are.	*indict those I've never heard of before*
810	To-morow I wyll aquyt them, yff nede were.	
	Thys lede I my lyff.	*Thus*
WYLL	Ye, but of us thre I have lest care.	*least*
	Met and drynke and ease, I aske no mare,	*Food*
	And a praty wench, to se here bare!	*pretty; see her*
815	I reke but lytyll be sche mayde or wyffe.	*I don't care*

MYNDE	Thys on a soper	*[I'll put] this [coin]; supper*
	I wyll be seen rycher,	
	Set a noble wyth goode chere	*Put forth*
	Redyly to spende.	
UNDYRSTONDYNGE	And I tweyn, be this feer,	*two [nobles]; company*
821	To moque at a goode dyner.	*enjoy ourselves*
	I hoope of a goode yer,	
	For ever I trost Gode wyll send.	

WYLL	And best we have wyne,	
825	Ande a cosyn of myn	
	Wyth us for to dyne.	
	Thre nobles wyll I spende frely.	*Three gold coins*
MYNDE	We shall acorde well and fyne.	
UNDYRSTONDYNGE	Nay, I wyll not passe schylyngys nyne.	*spend more than*
WYLL	No, thou was never but a swyn.	*anything but*
831	I woll be holdyn jentyll, by Sent Audre of Ely!	*considered noble, by St. Audrey*

	Ande now in my mynde I have	
	My cosyn Jenet N., so Gode me save.	*(see note)*
	Sche mornyth wyth a chorle, a very knave,	*suffers; churl, a true*
835	And never kan be mery.	
	I pley me ther wen I lyst rave;	*want to*
	Than the chorle wyll here dysprave.	*Then the churl; slander her*
	How myght make hym thys to lawe,	*How I can take him to court over this*
	I wolde onys have hym in the wyrry.	*then; by the throat*

| MYNDE | For thys I kan a remedye: | *know* |
| 841 | I shall rebuk hym thus so dyspytuusly | *insultingly* |

That of hys lyff he shall wery
　　And quak for very fere.
Ande yff he wyll not leve therby,   *stop*
845　On hys bodye he shall abye   *pay for it*
Tyll he leve that jelousy.
　　Nay, suche chorlys I kan lere!   *churls; teach*

UNDYRSTONDYNGE　Nay, I kan better hym quytte: *repay*
Arest hym fyrst to pes for fyght,   *keep the peace for fighting*
850　Than in another schere hym endyght,   *county indict him*
　　He ne shall wete by wom ne howe!   *whom nor*
Have hym in the Marschalsi seyn aryght,   *appear in the Knight-Marshal's court*
Than to the Amralté, for they wyll byght,   *Lord Admiral's court; be severe*
A *prevenire facias* than have as tyght,   *A writ of praemunire facias; tightly*
855　Ande thou shalt hurle hym so that he shall have inow.   *harass; enough*

WYLL: Wat and thes wrongys be espyede?   *What if; noticed*
UNDYRSTONDYNGE　Wyth the crose and the pyll I shall wrye yt, *heads and tails; conceal*
That ther shall never man dyscrey yt   *So that; perceive*
859　That may me appeyere.   *So that I might have to appear before the court*
MYNDE　Ther ys no craft but we may trye it.
UNDYRSTONDYNGE　Mede stoppyt, be yt never so allyede.   *Bribery stops [the law]; well-connected*
WYLL　Wyth you tweyn wo ys replyede,   *whoever you reply to*
863　He may sey he hathe a schrewde seyer.   *clever lawyer*

MYNDE　Thou woldyst have wondyr of sleyghtys that be.   *at the tricks*
UNDYRSTONDYNGE　Thys make sume ryche and summe never thé.   *prosper*
WYLL　They must nedys grett goodys gett thee!
　　Now go we to the wyne!
MYNDE　In treuthe I grante, have at wyth thee!
UNDYRSTONDYNGE　Ande for a peny or to, I wyll not fle.
WYLL　Mery, mery, all mery than be we!
871　Who that us tarythe, curs have he and myn!   *delays*

　　[*Enter Wisdom.*]

WYSDOM　O thou Mynde, remembyr thee!
　　Turne thi weys, thou gost amyse.
Se what thi ende ys, thou myght not fle.
875　Dethe to every creature certen ys.
They that lyve well, they shall have blys;
　　Thay that endyn yll, they goo to hell!
I am Wysdom, sent to tell you thys.
　　Se in what stat thou doyst indwell.   *See; you dwell in*

MYNDE　To my mynde yt cummyth from farre   *It seems to me*
881　That doutles man shall dey!

Ande thes weys we go, we erre.   *If*

Undyrstondynge, wat do ye sey?   *what*

UNDYRSTONDYNGE   I sey, man, holde forthe thi wey!   *stay on your path*

885   The lyff we lede ys sekyr ynowe.   *secure enough*

I wyll no undyrstondynge shall lett my pley.   *hinder*

Wyll, frende, how seyst thou?

WYLL   I wyll not thynke theron, to Gode a vowe!

We be yit but tender of age.

890   Schulde we leve this lyve? Ya, whowe?   *life; how*

We may amende wen we be sage.   *change when; aged*

WYSDOM   Thus many on unabylythe hym to grace;   *one makes himself unfit for*

They wyll not loke, but slumber and wynke.   *sleep*

They take not drede before ther face,

895   Howe horryble ther synnys stynke.

Wen they be on the pyttys brynke,   *When; the edge of the pit*

Than shall they trymbull and quake for drede.

Yit Mynde, I sey, you bethynke   *consider*

In what perell ye be now! Take hede!

900   Se howe ye have dysvyguryde your soule!

Beholde yourselff; loke veryly in mynde!   *truly into your mind*

Here Anima apperythe in the most horrybull wyse [manner], foulere than a fende.

MYNDE   Out! I tremble for drede, by Sent Powle!   *St. Paul*

Thys ys fouler than ony fend.   *any*

WYSDOM   Wy art thou creature so onkynde,   *Why; unnatural*

905   Thus to defoule Godys own place

That was made so gloryus wythout ende?

Thou hast made the Devylls rechace.   *called up the Devil*

As many dedly synnys as ye have usyde,

So many devllys in your soule be.

910   Beholde wat ys therin reclusyde!   *what; hidden*

Alas, man, of thi Soule have pyté!

Here rennyt out from undyr the horrybyll mantyll of the Soull six small boys in the lyknes of devyllys and so retorne ageyn.

WYSDAM   What have I do? Why lovyste thou not me?   *done*

Why cherysyste thi enmye? Why hatyst thou thi frende?   *do you cherish your enemy*

Myght I have don ony more for thee?   *any*

915   But love may brynge drede to mynde.

Thou hast made thee a bronde of hell   *firebrand*

Whom I made the ymage of lyght.

Yff the Devll myght, he wolde thee qwell   *destroy*

But that mercy expellyt hys myght.   *Unless; drives away*
920   Wy doyst thou, Soule, me all dyspyght?   *Why; injure*
     Why gevyst thou myn enmy that I have wrought?   *give; that which*
     Why werkyst thou hys consell; by myn settys lyght?   *pay no attention to mine*
       Why hatyst thou vertu? Why lovyst that ys nought?   *that which is nothing*

MYNDE A, lorde, now I brynge to mynde
925   My horryble synnys and myn offens,
     I se how I have defoulyde the noble kynde   *see; defiled; nature*
     That was lyke to thee by intellygens.   *because of*
     Undyrstondynge, I schew to your presens
       Our lyff wyche that ys most synfull.   *life*
930   Sek you remedye, do your dylygens   *Seek*
     To clense the Soull wyche ys this foull.   *so foul*

UNDYRSTONDYNGE By you, Mynde, I have very knowenge   *true knowledge*
     That grettly Gode we have offendyde;
   Endles peyn worthyi be our dysyrvynge
935   Wyche be ourselff never may be amendyde   *by ourselves*
     Wythout Gode, in whom all ys comprehendyde.
       Therfor to hym let us resort —
     He lefte up them that be descendyde.   *lifts; have fallen*
       He ys resurreccyon and lyve; to hem, Wyll, resort!   *life*

WYLL My wyll was full gove to syne,   *given*
941   By wyche the Soule ys so abhomynable.
     I wyll retorne to Gode and new begynne
     Ande in hym gronde my wyll stable,   *ground*
     That of hys mercy he wyll me able   *enable*
945   To have the giffte of hys specyall grace,   *gift*
     How hys seke Soule may be recurable   *sick; curable*
       At the jugment before hys face.

ANIMA Than wyth you thre the Soule dothe crye,
     "Mercy, Gode!" Why change I nowte,   *not at all*
950 I that thus horryble in synne lye,
     Sythe Mynde, Wyll, and Undyrstondynge be brought   *Since*
     To have knowynge they ill wrought?   *did ill*
       What ys that shall make me clene?
     Put yt, Lorde, into my thowte!
955   Thi olde mercy let me remene.   *remember*

WYSDOM Thow the soule mynde take   *Although*
     Ande undyrstondynge of hys synnys allwey,
   Beynge in wyll, yt forsake,   *forsake it (sin)*
     Yit thes do not only synnys awey,   *alone [take]*
960   But very contrycyon, who that have may,   *true*

That ys purger and clenser of synne.
A tere of the ey, wyth sorow veray,   *tear; eye; true*
That rubbyt and waschyt the Soule wythin.   *scrubs and washes*

All the penance that may be wrought,
965   Ne all the preyer that seyde be kan,
Wythout sorowe of hert relesyt nought.   *remits nothing*
That in especyall reformyth man   *in particular*
Ande makyt hym as clene as when he begane.
Go seke this medsyne, Soull. That beseke   *seek; medicine*
970   Wyth veray feythe, and be ye sekyr than   *true; certain*
The vengeaunce of Gode ys made full meke.

By Undyrstondynge have very contrycyon,   *true*
Wyth Mynde of your synne confessyon make,
Wyth Wyll yeldynge du satysfaccyon.   *yielding*
975   Than your soule be clene, I undyrtake.   *will be; promise*
ANIMA I wepe for sorowe, Lorde! I begyn awake,
I that this longe hath slumberyde in syne.

Hic recedunt demones.   *Here the demons exit*

WYSDOM Lo, how contrycyon avoydyth the devllys blake!   *drives out*
Dedly synne ys non you wythin!

980   For Gode ye have offendyde hyghly
Ande your modyr, Holy Chyrche so mylde,
Therfor Gode ye must aske mercy,   *[of] God*
By Holy Chyrch to be reconsylyde,
Trustynge verely ye shall never be revylyde   *truly; reviled*
985   Yff ye have your charter of pardon by confessyon.
Now have ye forgeffnes that were fylyde.   *defiled*
Go prey your modyr Chyrche of her proteccyon.

ANIMA O Fadyr of mercy ande of comfort,
Wyth wepynge ey and hert contryte   *eye*
990   To our modyr, Holy Chyrche, I wyll resort,
My lyff pleyn schewenge to here syght.   *My life openly displayed*
Wyth Mynde, Undyrstondynge, and Wyll ryght,
Wyche of my Soull the partyes be,   *parts*
To the domys of the Chyrche we shall us dyght,   *judgement; put*
995   Wyth veray contricyon thus compleynnyng we.   *lamenting*

*Here they go out, and in the goynge the Soule syngyth in the most lamentabull wyse [manner],
wyth drawte notys [long drawn-out notes] as yt ys songyn in the passyon wyke [Easter Week]:*

ANIMA   *Magna velud mare contricio, contricio tua: quis consoletur tui?*
          Plorans ploravit in nocte, et lacrime ejus in maxillis ejus.[1]

WYSDOM   Thus seth Gode mankynde tyll   *saith; to*
             The nyne poyntys ples hym all other before.
1000 "Gyff a peny in thy lyve wyth goode wyll
             To the pore, and that plesythe Gode more
             Than mouyntenys into golde tramposyde wore   *mountains; converted*
                 Ande aftyr thy dethe for thee dysposyde."   *spent for your sake*
             Ande all the goodys thou hast in store
1005   Shulde not profyght so moche wan thi body ys closyde.   *when; buried*

             The secunde poynt, Gode sethe thus,
             "Wepe on tere for my love hertyly,   *one*
             Or for the passyon of me, Jhesus,
             Ande that plesyt me more specyally
1010   Than yff thou wepte for thi frendys or goodys worldly
                 As moche water as the se conteynys."   *sea*
             Lo, contrycyon ys a soveren remedy   *supreme*
                 That dystroythe synnys, that relessyt peynys.   *sets [the soul] free from pains*

             The thyrde, Gode sethe, "Suffyr pacyenly for my love   *patiently*
1015   Of thi neybure a worde of repreve,   *neighbor; reproof*
             Ande that to mercy mor dothe me move
                 Than thou dyscyplynyde thi body wyth peynys greve   *grievous pains*
                 Wyth as many roddys as myght grow or thryve
                     In the space of a days jornyé."   *journey*
1020   Lo, who suffyryth most for Gode ys most leve,   *dear*
                 Slandyr, repreve, ony adversyté.   *any*

             The fourte, Gode sethe, "Wake on ouyr for the love of me,   *Keep a vigil one hour*
             And that to me ys more plesaunce
             Than yff thou sent twelve kyngys free   *noble*
1025   To my sepulkyr wyth grett puysschaunce   *force*
             For my dethe to take vengeaunce."
                 Lo, wakynge ys a holy thynge.   *keeping vigil*
                 Ther yt ys hade wyth goode usance,   *done properly*
                     Many gracys of yt doth sprynge.

1030 The fyfte, Gode sethe, "Have pyté and compassyon
                 Of thi neybur wyche ys seke and nedy,
             And that to me ys more dylectacyon
                 Than thou fastyde forty yer by and by   *continually*

----

[1] Lines 996–97: *Greater than the sea is your breach, your contrition; what can comfort you? / She weeps sore in the night, and her tears are on her cheeks* (Lamentations 2:13 and 1:2)

Thre days in the weke, as streytly   *strictly*
1035   As thou cowdys in water and brede."   *could*
Lo, pyté God plesyth grettly,
        Ande yt ys a vertu soveren, as clerkys rede.   *supreme*

The sixte, Gode seth on this wyse,
        "Refreyn thy speche for my reverens,   *Restrain*
1040 Lett not thy tonge thy eveyn-Crysten dyspyse,   *fellow-Christians slander*
        Ande than plesyst thou more myn excellens
        Than yff thou laberyde wyth grett dylygens
                Upon thy nakyde feet and bare
        Tyll the blode folwude for peyn and vyolens   *flowed*
1045   Ande aftyr eche stepe yt sene were."   *visible*

The sevente, Cryst seth in this maner,
        "Thy neybur to evyll ne sterre not thou,   *incite*
But all thynge torne into vertu chere,   *virtuous behavior*
        And than more plesyst thou me now
1050   Then yf a thousende tymys thou renne thorow   *run through*
        A busche of thornys that scharpe were
        Tyll thi nakyde body were all rough
        Ande evyn rent to the bonys bare."   *torn*

The eyghte, Gode sethe this man till,   *to man*
1055   "Oftyn pray and aske of me,
        And that plesythe me more onto my wyll
        Than yf my modyr and all sentys preyde for thee."

The nynte, God sethe, "Love me soverenly,   *above all else*
        Ande that to me more plesant ys
1060 Than yf thou went upon a pyler of tre   *wooden pillar*
        That wer sett full of scharpe prykkys   *spikes*
        So that thou cut thi flesche into the smale partys."   *little pieces*
                Lo, Gode ys plesyde more wyth the dedys of charyté
        Than all the peynys man may suffer iwys.   *pains; indeed*
1065   Remembyr thes poyntys, man, in thi felycité!

Here entrethe Anima, wyth the Fyve Wyttys [Senses] goynge before, Mynde on the on [one] syde
and Undyrstondynge on the other syde and Wyll folowyng, all in here fyrst clothynge, her
chapplettys [coronets] and crestys [badges], and all havyng on crownys, syngynge in here [their]
commynge in: "Quid retribuam Domino pro omnibus que retribuit mihi? Calicem salutaris
accipiam et nomen Domini invocabo."[1]

---

[1] Line 1065, s.d.: *What can I render to the Lord for all that he has given me? I will take the cup of*
salvation and call upon the name of the Lord (Psalm 115:12–13)

ANIMA O meke Jhesu, to thee I crye!

O swet Jhesu, my delectacyon!   *delight*

O Jhesu, the sune of Vyrgyne Marye,   *son*

Full of mercy and compassyon!

1070   My soule ys waschede by thy passyon

Fro the synnys cummynge by sensualyté.   *From*

A, be thee I have a new resurreccyon.   *through thee*

The lyght of grace I fele in me.   *feel*

In tweyn myghtes of my soule I thee offendyde: *two powers*

1075   The on by my inwarde wyttys, thow ben gostly;   *one; those which are spiritual*

The other by my outwarde wyttys comprehendyde,

Tho be the fyve wyttys bodyly,   *Those; senses*

Wyth the wyche tweyn myghtys mercy I crye.   *two powers*

My modyr, Holy Chyrche, hath gove me grace,   *given*

1080   Whom ye fyrst toke to your mercy,

Yet of myselff I may not satysfye my trespas.   *on my own*

Magna est misericordia tua!   *Your mercy is great*

Wyth full feyth of foryevenes to thee, Lorde, I come.   *forgiveness*

WYSDOM *Vulnerasti cor meum, soror mea, sponsa,*

1085   *In uno ictu oculorum tuorum.*[1]

Ye have wondyde my hert, syster, spouse dere,   *wounded*

In the tweyn syghtys of your ey,   *two glances*

By the recognycyon ye have clere,   *acknowledgment; clearly*

Ande by the hye love ye have godly.

1090   It perrysschyt my hert to here you crye,   *destroys*

Now ye have forsake synne and be contryte.

Ye were never so leve to me verelye.   *dear; truly*

Now be ye reformyde to your bewtys bryght.   *returned; beauty*

Ande ther your fyve wyttys offendyde has,   *senses; have*

1095   Ande to mak asythe be impotent,   *atonement are*

My fyve wyttys, that never dyde trespas   *senses*

Hathe made asythe to the Father suffycyent.   *atonement*

Wyth my syght I se the people vyolent,   *see*

I herde hem vengeaunce onto me call,

1100   I smelte the stenche of caren here present,   *carrion*

I tastyde the drynke mengylde wyth gall.   *mixed*

By touchynge I felte peyns smerte,   *sharp*

My handys sprede abrode to halse thi swyre,   *embrace thy neck*

---

[1] Lines 1084–85: *You have ravished my heart, my sister, my spouse, / With one glance of your eyes* (Canticles 4:9)

	My fete naylyde to abyde wyth thee, swet herte,	
1105	My hert clovyn for thi love most dere.	*split*
	Myn hede bowhede down to kys thee here,	
	My body full of holys as a dovehous.	*as full of holes*
	In thys ye be reformyde, Soule, my plesere,	*restored*
	Ande now ye be the very temple of Jhesus.	

1110	Fyrst ye were reformyde by baptyme of ygnorans	*restored by baptism*
	And clensyde from the synnys orygynall.	
	Ande now ye be reformyde by the sakyrment of penance	*restored*
	Ande clensyde from the synnys actuall.	
	Now ye be fayrest, Crystys own specyall!	
1115	Dysfygure you never to the lyknes of the fende!	*Do not disfigure yourself*
	Now ye have receyvyde the crownnys victoryall	*crowns of victory*
	To regne in blys wythoutyn ende.	

MYNDE	Have mynde, Soule, wat Gode hath do,	*what; done*
	Reformyde you in feyth veryly.	*Restored; truly*
1120	*Nolite conformari huic seculo*	
	Sed reformamini in novitate spiritus sensus vestri:[1]	
	Conforme you not to this pompyus glory	*ostentatious*
	But reforme in gostly felynge.	*spiritual*
	Ye that were dammyde by synn endelesly,	
1125	Mercy hathe reformyde you ande crownyde as a kynge.	

UNDYRSTONDYNGE	Take understondynge, Soule, now ye	
	Wyth contynuall hope in Godys behest.	
	Renovamini spiritu mentis vestre	
	Et induite novum hominem, qui secundum Deum creatus est:[2]	
1130	Ye be reformyde in felynge, not only as a best,	*beast*
	But also in the over parte of your reasun,	*higher*
	Be wyche ye have lyknes of Gode mest	*most*
	Ande of that mercyfull very cognycyon.	*true knowledge*

WYLL	Now the Soule yn charyté reformyde ys,	
1135	Wyche charyté ys Gode verely.	*truly*
	Exspoliantem veterem hominem cum actibus suis:	
	Et induite novum qui renovatur in agnicionem dei.[3]	
	Spoyll you of your olde synnys and foly	*Divest yourself*

---

[1] Lines 1120–21: *Be not conformed to this world, / But be transformed by the renewing of your spiritual senses* (Romans 12:2)

[2] Lines 1128–29: *Be renewed in the spirit of your mind, / And put on the new man, created in God's likeness* (Ephesians 4:23–24)

[3] Lines 1136–37: *I would put away the old man with his deeds, / And clothe yourself like a new man in the knowledge of God* (Colossians 3:9)

Ande be renuyde in Godys knowynge ageyn,   *restored; knowledge*
1140   That enduyde wyth grace so specyally,   *That is endowed*
Conservynge in peyn, ever in blys for to reyn.   *reign*

ANIMA   Then wyth you thre I may sey this
Of Our Lorde, soveren person, Jhesus:
Suavis est Dominus universis,
1145   *Et miseraciones ejus super omnia opera ejus.*[1]
O thou hye soveren Wysdam, my joy, Cristus,
Hevyn, erthe, and eche creature
Yelde you reverens, for grace pleyntuus   *plentiful*
Ye geff to mann, ever to induyr.   *give; last*

1150 Now wyth Sent Powle we may sey thus   *St. Paul*
That be reformyde thorow feyth in Jhesum,
We have peas and acorde betwyx Gode and us,   *peace*
Justificati ex fide pacem habemus ad Deum.[2]
Now to Salamonys conclusyon I com: *Solomon's*
1155   *Timor Domini inicium sapiencie.*[3]
[WISDOM]   *Vobis qui timetis Deum*
Orietur sol justicie.[4]

The tru son of ryghtusnes,
Wyche that ys Our Lorde Jhesu,
1160 Shall sprynge in hem that drede hys meknes.
Nowe ye mut every soule renewe   *must*
In grace, and vycys to eschew.   *vices*
Ande so to ende wyth perfeccyon,
That the doctryne of Wysdom we may sew: *follow*
1165   *Sapiencia Patris*, graunt that for hys passyon!   *The Wisdom of the Father*
AMEN!

---

[1] Lines 1144–45: *The Lord is good to all, / And his tender mercies are over all his works* (Psalm 144:9)

[2] *Being justified by faith, we have peace with God* (Romans 5:1)

[3] *The fear of the Lord is the beginning of wisdom* (Proverbs 1:7).

[4] Lines 1156–57: *To you who fear the Lord / Shall the sun of righteousness arise* (Malachias 4:2)

 NOTES TO WISDOM

ABBREVIATIONS: *CA*: Gower, *Confessio Amantis*; *CT*: Chaucer, *Canterbury Tales*; **D**: Oxford, Bodleian Library MS Digby 133; *MED*: *Middle English Dictionary*; **M**: Macro Manuscript, Washington DC; *OED*: *Oxford English Dictionary*; **s.d.**: stage direction; **Tilley:** Tilley, *Dictionary of Proverbs in England*; **Whiting**: Whiting, *Proverbs, Sentences, and Proverbial Phrases*.

1, s.d.   Wisdom's elaborate costume is composed almost entirely of elements whose use was restricted to royalty by sumptuary laws, and the orb and scepter which he holds confirm his identification as a regal figure. Contemporary art would also identify Wisdom as Christ in majesty, an equation for which there is ample scriptural tradition (see, for example, Isaias 11:1–2, 1 Corinthians 1:24, or Luke 11:49). Wisdom's description of the Crucifixion at the end of the play (lines 1096–1107) confirms his identification with Christ.

16, s.d.   *chappelet*. M: *chappetelot*, Eccles' emendation. Anima's costume is symbolic of the dual nature of man's soul, at once divine and sinful. Her furred white garment, representing the soul's eternal and divine nature, is covered with a black mantle indicating its fallen state; a coronet or small crown indicates her nobility.

17   *Hanc amavi et exquisivi*. The passage is from the Wisdom of Solomon, one of the "deuterocanonical" books of the Bible, which differ from the "canonical" books in that they do not occur in the Hebrew Bible. Anima cites the first line of the passage in Latin, but her speech continues to translate the text: "Hanc amavi et exquisivi a iuventute mea, et quaesivi sponsam mihi adsumere et amator factus sum formae illius" [Her have I loved, and have sought her out from my youth, and have desired to take for my spouse, and I became a lover of her beauty]. The playwright is clearly not concerned by the (unequivocally) female Anima speaking a passage directed in its scriptural source to a female lover.

25   *Of*. M: *Off*. Here, as elsewhere, I have transcribed *ff* as *f* to avoid confusion between the of/off prepositions.

63–64   This sentiment echoes the spiritual belief of St. Bonaventure in *The Mind's Road to God*, as well as in the anonymous *Cloud of Unknowing*, wherein God is only knowable through experience, and that experience cannot be put into words.

103–06   Wisdom describes the creation of man in God's image as it appears in Genesis 1:27 and following, prior to Adam's offence, as described in Genesis 3:6–19.

111   The "original sin" of which Wisdom speaks describes the fallen state of man following Adam and Eve's expulsion from the Garden of Eden. Although all

men and women have not individually committed the sin of Adam and Eve, their sin and expulsion is directly responsible for man's fallen state. As Paul explained the doctrine, "For as by one man's disobedience many were made sinners, so by the obedience of one shall many be made righteous" (Romans 5:19).

124   *the sacramentys sevyn.* Although Wisdom refers to the seven sacraments, he only specifically mentions baptism. The others are eucharist, confession, confirmation, marriage, ordination of priests, and extreme unction (also called anointing of the sick).

134   Although the character of Anima is clearly feminine and is portrayed as the bride of Wisdom/Christ, the sources (especially those in Latin) are ambiguous about the soul's gender, and occasional masculine pronouns slip into the text, especially when the soul is presented in its regal capacity. See also lines 147 and, especially, 289 and 1125. "He" sometimes, however, designates either male or female (e.g., *Pride of Life*, line 68).

178   The association of the soul's three faculties with the Trinity derives from St. Augustine's treatise *De Trinitate* (Book xv, chapter 23), in which Mind, Understanding, and Will are associated respectively with the Father, Son, and Holy Ghost.

183–212   Mind is showing off here with elaborate word-play on his name. He is mindful of the frailty of his mind, but it is his mind which leads him to God, whom he asks to be mindful of him.

269–74   The equation of God and charity (divine love) is a commonplace of medieval theology. Although repeated by virtually all writers, the most frequently cited source for the idea is St. Augustine's *De doctrina christiana*, though the initial source is likely such passages as "Deus caritas est" (God is love) in 1 John 4.8.

276   The "tabernacle" is the human body which has been created in God's image ("lyknes," line 274). God "rests" in man as an indication of the divine nature of his soul.

294   The traditional three enemies of Mankind, the World, the Flesh, and the Devil, appear in several other plays as well, notably in the Digby play of Mary Magdalene and *The Castle of Perseverance*. Though the idea — a sort of evil parallel to the Trinity — was widespread, it may derive ultimately from the *Meditations* attributed to St. Bernard of Clairvaux, Chapter 12, "De tribus inimicis hominis, carne, mundo, et diabolo" ("On the Three Enemies of Man, the Flesh, the World, and the Devil"). See also Wenzel, "Three Enemies of Man."

321   The story of the oil of mercy is apocryphal, and its primary source is the Gospel of Nichodemus, which also tells the story of the Harrowing of Hell. According to the apocryphal account, immediately following the expulsion from the Garden of Eden, Adam is given a promise that at the end of his life he would receive the oil of mercy. At the age of 130, Adam asks his third son Seth, an obedient son born long after the killing of Abel, to go to Paradise for the promised oil of mercy. Seth travels to Paradise, where the archangel Michael allows him a vision of Paradise. Incorporated into the vision is the image of a child, whom Michael identifies as the coming Christ, who is the promised oil of

mercy. For the full text, see Kim, *Gospel of Nichodemus*, pp. 37–38 (Latin); or James, *Apocryphal New Testament*, pp. 126–28 (English translation).

324, s.d.   Lucifer is "disguised": his devil's costume "without" covers a gallant's flamboyant clothing "within," so that his costume change at line 408 simply involves removing the devil's attire. The description here suggests that the gallant's dress may be at least partially visible beneath the devil costume. Beside this stage direction a hand different from that of the text has marked a cross in the left margin; such marginal crosses also appear at twenty-six other places in the text, eleven of them opposite stage directions. John Marshall has suggested that they may have been a production aid, perhaps indicating significant changes of stage-picture. See Marshall, "Marginal Staging Marks."

325   "Out, harrow" is a frequent cry of the devils in the biblical plays, generally signifying anger and frustration, though it is also the reaction of the poor widow and her daughters to the fox's capture of Chaunteclere in Chaucer's Nun's Priest's Tale (*CT* VII[B²]4570).

327–28   *My place to restore, / God hath made man!* The plays commonly assert the proposition that mankind was created to fill the gap left when Satan and his horde of angels fell. E.g., York Cycle 7.23–24, 37.13–16; and N-Town 11.48 ff. (Parliament of Heaven). See also Gower, *CA* 8.30–36 and *Cursor Mundi* 514–16. The idea figures prominently in St. Augustine's *Enchiridion*, ch. 29.

341–42   Lucifer's "wyly . . . knowynge," that is worldly knowledge, is a direct contrast to a very different kind of knowledge, the wisdom represented by Christ.

343   *compleccyons.* Elemental humors of the body (melancholy, bile, choler, phlegm) through which humankind is especially vulnerable.

380, s.d.   See note to line 324, s.d.; although the stage direction indicates that Lucifer goes offstage to remove his devil costume, there is no practical reason why he must do so. Perhaps he simply steps behind a curtain in order to deposit his now superfluous attire.

381–92   As Riggio has pointed out, these opening speeches of the returning Mights indicate a clear differentiation of intellect: Mind, representing higher reason and therefore the most intellectual, is concerned with studying God's *doctrine*; Understanding, representing lower worldly reason, will follow God's *law*; and Will, representing sense and passion, will offer God *praise*. See Riggio, *Play of Wisdom*, pp. 229–30.

394   Lucifer's first attack on the three Mights is based on a quotation from Scripture, hinting at the way he will twist theological arguments to his own purpose.

401   Again, Lucifer refers to a scriptural passage which the audience (and the three Mights) would undoubtedly recognize (Ecclesiastes 3:1–3).

413   *Mertha.* Martha, the sister of Mary and Lazarus. See Luke 10:38–42. During the Middle Ages, she was regarded as typifying the active life. See Aquinas, *Catena Aurea*, Luke 10:38–42.

414   *Maria.* Maria is the contemplative sister of Martha, who typifies the active life.
           (See Luke 10:38–42.) The activities of Martha please God greatly (line 413)
           but Maria pleases God more, since the "Contemplatyff lyff ys sett befor" (line
           417). This Mary was traditionally identified with Mary Magdalene. See the
           Digby Mary Magdalene play.

428   How one reads Lucifer's arguments in favor of the "mixed life" is crucial in the
           context of interpreting the play as a whole. A life which combined contemplation
           with living in the world (as opposed to a strictly cloistered life) was often held up
           as an ideal, as the mode of life which Christ himself led (lines 419–28). If the
           three Mights, as their arguments would suggest, are presented as cloistered
           monks, Lucifer's arguments could be seen as more effective than advice to aban-
           don contemplation entirely. Much of the argument is derived from Walter
           Hilton's fourteenth-century treatise *On the Mixed Life*, and David Bevington has
           suggested that the playwright is in fact arguing in favor of the mixed life despite
           presenting the case in the voice of Lucifer, since Lucifer's arguments represent
           a substantial distortion of Hilton's explanation (*Macro Plays*, p. xiii).

431 ff.   Lucifer's success at seducing Mind through logical argument is signaled by
           Mind's admission that Lucifer has "reason" (line 445).

433   Lucifer's warning against the difficulties of the contemplative life echoes the
           advice given by Thomas à Kempis, *De imitatione Christi*, Book 1, chapter 19.4:
           "Numquam sis ex toto otiosus, sed aut legens, aut scribens, aut orans, aut
           meditans, aut aliquid utilitatis pro communi laborans" (Never be completely
           idle, but either reading or writing, or praying or meditating, or at some useful
           work for the common good).

445   *me seme ye have reson.* Lucifer's arguments against the contemplative life and
           his rejection of "harde lyvynge, and goynge wyth dyscyplyne dew" (line 434,
           as well as Mind's defense of the contemplative life, line 446) imply that the
           three Mights are dressed as contemplatives.

451–56   Lucifer's seduction of Understanding is centered on the offer of power and
           authority as well as their outward signs, that is, fine clothing. Lucifer appeals to
           Understanding's five wits as a source of "delectacyon," as well as the "domi-
           nacyon" or power inherent in those who dress well and present an authoritative
           aspect.

468   Lucifer's twisted discussion of what best pleases God may be the catalyst for Wis-
           dom's concluding sermon on the Nine Virtues, lines 998–1065.

473–76   *What synne ys in met? In ale? In wyn? / Wat synne ys in ryches? In clothynge fyne? / All
           thynge Gode ordenyde to man to inclyne. / Leve your nyse chastyté, and take a wyff!*
           Lucifer offers Will the physical pleasures of the senses, good food and drink,
           wealth, and sex. Since Will is not much given to logical argument, he falls easily.

479   Wisdom has already warned against basing conclusions solely on the informa-
           tion of the five senses (lines 295–300).

488   Riggio (*Play of Wisdom*, p. 243) suggests that "thes prechors" might well refer to members of the audience. This would certainly accord with Lucifer's other interactions with the audience (lines 433–40, 490, and possibly 518).

490   The line could be directed at a clerical member of the audience.

492   *sett my soule on a mery pynne.* The phrase is proverbial, and appears in other plays, such as Henry Medwall's *Nature* (lines 865 and 1084). See Whiting, P215, and Tilley, P335. A "pynne" is a peg, perhaps of a musical instrument, and the phrase means to "direct one's thoughts towards pleasure."

494   Throughout his conversation with the three Mights, Lucifer has been directly subverting the arguments of Wisdom which opened the play; here he concludes by redefining the "clene soull" (which Wisdom had identified as "Godys restynge place," line 193) as "mery."

510   *Change that syde aray.* Lucifer advises Mind to change his long gown ("syde aray"), presumably for a shorter, more fashionable coat. A primary focus of anti-fashion satire in the fifteenth century was the short coat which provided little protection from the elements but displayed the wearer's attributes to advantage. So in *Mankind*, Newguise disapproves of Mankind's practical "syde gown" and recommends replacing it with a "jakett" (lines 671–72).

511   The meaning here is a bit unclear, signaled by the very different readings in the two manuscripts ("and it hap" in Digby, "hanip" in Macro). "La plu joly" would seem to be the name of a song. The Digby reading might mean "if it happen [to the tune of . . .]."

513–15   The idea figures prominently in St. Augustine's *Enchiridion* 29, entitled "The Restored Part of Humanity Shall, in Accordance with the Promises of God, Succeed to the Place Which the Rebellious Angels Lost."

522   *Resone I have made both deff and dumme.* Lucifer has perverted reason, making it "deff and dumme." As he gloats about his success in the seduction of the three Mights, he indicates precisely the three sins to which they will be subject: Mind will be governed by Pride, the principal sin of the intellect; Understanding by Avarice or Covetousness, the principal sin of worldliness; and Will by Lechery, the principal sin of the physical body.

530–31   Covetousness is the sin to which Humanum Genus ("Mankind") succumbs at the end of his life in *Castle of Perseverance* (lines 2700 ff.).

542   *Wyll clenness ys in mankyn.* M: *Wyll clennes ys mankyn.* Neither Davis nor Bevington emend. Coldeway suggests "Wyll in clenness ys mankyn," but the *Wisdom*-playwright would not be likely to use such inverted diction.

549, s.d. The naughty boy whom Lucifer carries off with him might be a plant by the acting company or a mischievous and annoying child in the audience. Although several editions of the play gloss "boy" as "young man," it would be important for the victim to be small enough to be picked up and carried with relative ease. Lucifer's abduction of an annoying child is intended as a warning to the audience of his power over them.

550–61   Each of the Mights indicates that his new relationship to Lucifer is displayed physically by new (and fashionable) clothes.

551   *Wyppe, wyrre, care awey!* The interjections here (and at 762 and 890) are clear enough in their general sense, though their exact meaning is uncertain. They may well simply be expressions of pleasure or, in the latter two cases, of alarm.

601   Simony, the buying or selling of church offices for profit, was a substantial problem in the Middle Ages, when many churchmen held temporal administrative positions in addition to their spiritual positions within the church. Dante's *Inferno* condemned the simoniacs to the eighth circle of Hell. A fourteenth-century poem "The Simonie," linking simony and covetousness or greed, is found in Dean, *Medieval English Political Writings*, pp. 193–212.

602–03   This definition of falseness as wisdom is, of course, the inversion on which the play turns: true wisdom (that is oneness with Christ) has been perverted into worldly wisdom (that is falseness and deceit).

616–18   Several three-part drinking songs survive in the Fayrfax and Ritson manuscripts (British Library MS Add. 5465 and 5665 respectively, both edited by John Stevens in *Early Tudor Songs and Carols*). The Powers identify their parts: Will is the treble or top part, Understanding the mean or middle part, and Mind the tenor or lower part.

632–35   Mind presents, in effect, a definition of Maintenance, the character he will adopt in the first dance. Described by Bevington as "the chief legal abuse of the age," Maintenance involved the support or "maintaining" of a large body of liveried retainers for the specific purpose of interfering in legal proceedings. Maintenance represented a defiance of the central authority of the law, and both Richard III and Henry VII passed legislation intended to restrict its abuse. See Bevington, *Tudor Drama and Politics*, p. 30. The closest modern equivalent would likely be "graft" or "obstruction of justice."

636–43   Whereas Mind's perversion of the legal system was aimed at gaining power and authority ("myghty lordeschyppe," line 629) in support of his sin of Pride, Understanding will use the courts for financial gain to satisfy his sin of Avarice. His methods will include simony (the selling of ecclesiastical offices, see note to line 601) and bribery.

684   A marginal note at this point reads "va . . ." which is completed at line 784 with ". . . cat" (also in the margin). The word "vacat" ("it may be omitted") in the same hand as the playtext clearly indicates that the scribe envisioned more than one performance, with the possibility of omitting the dances (and thus eliminating the need for eighteen dancers). Such an omission might anticipate a smaller venue, a less costly performance, or a performance intended for touring. The initial direction ("va . . .") also appears in the Digby manuscript; the closing direction would presumably have appeared in the section of the manuscript which is now lost.

691, s.d. The dancers are "dysgysed" (masked) and are dressed in the "sute" or livery of Mind. Their costuming is based on images of power and authority: red beards, lions rampant (standing upright, usually upon one hind leg, in a position of attack), and carrying clubs or batonlike weapons. Each of the Mights is followed by six named dancers costumed identically (or, in the case of Lechery, in two gendered groups of three), and these followers associate their leader directly with one of the three traditional enemies of mankind: the World, the Flesh, and the Devil. Mind/Maintenance is followed by representatives of the Devil's sins, Pride, Envy, and Wrath (line 752).

696   *discorde.* M *dycorde*; reading from D.

697   Lovedays defined periods of time during which lawsuits and other legal matters might be settled out of court as well as the agreements made on such occasions. See Bennett, "Mediaeval Loveday."

706   "Madame Regent" is likely to be the name of the dance which the trumpets play, but it is unknown. Very little dance music survives from late fifteenth-century England, although a recently discovered manuscript in the Derbyshire Record Office associated with the Gresley family gives the tenors for eight dances over which the players would improvise one or more parts. See Fallows, "Gresley Dance Collection." One possible reconstruction of these dances can be found online at <www.hants.gov.uk/basdance/gresley.html>.

717   Cloaked Collusion, one of the Vices in John Skelton's *Magnyfycence* (printed around 1530), says that he himself bears "two faces in a hood" (line 710).

720   The inquest or jury of Holborn; the district of Holborn was well known as the legal quarter of London, housing not only the law schools and the Inns of Court but also the Fleet Prison.

723, s.d.   Understanding/Perjury's dancers wear "hattys of Meyntenance," that is, they are liveried indicating their allegiance to a patron. His followers each represent qualities used to gain advantage in a legal suit and thus to accumulate wealth through fraud.

730   *evyll endyrecte.* So D. M reads *entyrecte*, which Eccles glosses as "ointment." I have followed D here, as does Riggio, who translates "evil twist."

740   This sounds like a proverb, though it is not recorded as such. It might be a variant of the proverb "There goes the hare away," Whiting H120 and Tilley H157. Whiting discusses the use of proverbs in the play in *Proverbs in the Earlier English Drama*, pp. 75–77.

751, s.d.   There seems to be no ambiguity about Will/Lechery's dancers: they are six women, three of them cross-dressed as gallants. Although it is frequently claimed that women did not appear on the stage in England until after the Restoration, there is clear evidence of female performers in the Middle Ages. See Brown and Parolin, *Women Players in England,* where a number of the essays assume the existence of female performers prior to 1500. Also, these women are dancers rather than actors, and records of female dancers are common in the fifteenth century. The meaning of "conregent" is not clear. The base meaning would seem to be "ruling together" (as the *OED* gives it) or "having the same author-ity," so it likely indicates that they wear the same livery. A hornpipe is a wind instrument constructed at least partially of animal horn, thus representing here an image of cuckoldry. Animal horns were used in the construction of several kinds of instruments, including bagpipes, fipple flutes (like recorders), and pibcorns.

758   "Bete," or "Betty," would seem to be a generic name for a loose woman.

762   The exact meaning of the interjection is uncertain, and it may simply be an expression of surprise (see also 551 and 890).

764 ff.   The dance degenerates into a fight between the three Mights, symbolic of the discord and lack of order into which they have fallen after their seduction by Lucifer.

775, s.d.   It is Wyll's six dancers who leave (the "dumb show"), not the three Mights.

783   *by the bon.* A relatively mild oath, a less offensive variant of "By God's bones." It may also have a phallic overtone, since Wyll has now become Lechery.

788   Westminster Hall (just north of Westminster Abbey, near the present site of the Houses of Parliament) was the venue for three of the most important courts: King's Bench, Common Pleas, and Chancery. In the moral interlude *Hick Scorner* (c. 1514), Imagination claims: "And yet I can imagine things subtle / For to get money plenty. / In Westminster Hall every term I am" (Lancashire, *Two Tudor Interludes*, lines 215–17).

792–93   The area around St. Paul's was a center for the conduct of business, both com-mercial and legal, centering on the parvise, the enclosed and covered area at the west door. Writing during Elizabeth I's reign, William Harrison notes that "[t]he time hath been that our lawyers did sit in Paul's upon stools against the pillars and walls to get clients" (*Description of England*, p. 174).

803   *engrose.* M: *engose*, Eccles' emendation.

808   *nether.* M: *nther*, Riggio's emendation.

818   A noble was worth 6 s. 8 d, or one third of a pound.

831   St. Audrey was the common anglicization of the Anglo-Saxon St. Etheldreda, founder (in 673) and patron saint of the cathedral at Ely; the London resi-dence of the bishop of Ely was on Ely Place, just at the east end of the district of Holborn, next to a church dedicated to St. Etheldreda.

833   *N.* likely stands for *nomen* (name) and the performer would insert the last name of someone local or a member of the audience.

849–50   Having a person arrested in one county (shire) while indicting him in another county at the same time was an effective means of guaranteeing his conviction. Since he would have been required to be present at both hearings, his absence at one would ensure his conviction at the second.

852	The Marshalsea Court was held before the king's steward and knight-marshal, and dealt primarily with cases involving members of the royal household as well as with cases involving trespass in the vicinity of royal property.
853	The High Court of the Admiralty was given jurisdiction under Edward III over a variety of acts committed at sea, including piracy and ownership of wrecks. Its jurisdiction seems to have expanded quickly to include a variety of civil disputes, since legislation was found to be necessary under both Richard II and Henry IV to restrain the spread of the High Court's actions.
854	A writ of *praemunire facias* ("you shall warn"; the manuscript reading is incorrect) required the sheriff to summon someone accused of pursuing a suit in a foreign country which should be pursued in an English court.
857	*the crose and the pyll*. From the French *la croix et la pile*, the phrase refers to the two sides of a coin, exactly equivalent to "heads and tails."
870	The frequent use of the word "mery" following the fall of the Mights gives it a strong association with their sinful, revelous state.
890	*whowe*. The exact meaning of the interjection is uncertain, and it may simply be an expression of disbelief, like "whoa" (see also 551 and 762).
900	*dysvyguryde*. M: *dyvyguryde*, Eccles' emendation. At line 697 the M scribe appears to have misread D's *discorde* as *dycorde*, and it is possible that he has made the same mistake here, though without this page of D it is not possible to tell.
907	A *rechace* is the call that is sounded to muster the hounds for a hunt; the "sounds" of the three Mights have called the Devil.
911, s.d.	The manuscript reads "vi small boys" but this is likely a scribal error for "vii," since Wisdom explicitly connects them (line 979) with the Seven Deadly Sins. Riggio, following the events of the Mights' masque dances, suggests that Anima is to be taken as the seventh devil in the same way that each of the Mights becomes a seventh along with his six dancers. The equation of Anima with one of the Seven Deadly Sins would, however, be theologically inappropriate.
934	*dysyrvynge*. M: *dysyrynge*, Eccles' emendation. This may be another case of M misreading an "I" if D's reading was *dysyrvinge*.
972–74	*very contrycyon*. Wisdom outlines the traditional form of penance, defined as contrition, or sorrow of heart; confession to an appropriate ecclesiastical authority; and satisfaction or restitution. This explanation appears in a wide variety of sources, among them Hilton's *Scale of Perfection* (see Appendix 1).
985	*your charter*. The playwright's image of a formal charter which the penitent soul receives through confession likely comes from Hilton's *Scale of Perfection* (see Appendix 1).
988	*comfort*. M: *mercy*, Eccles' emendation.
999	The Nine Points (*Novem Virtutes*) are described in several fifteenth-century texts in both Latin and English, and in both prose and verse. The English versions

are not as close to *Wisdom* as the Latin prose text printed in Appendix 1, pp. 89–90. In general, the nine points involve a personal and emotional commitment to God, rather than a formal or public involvement. As such, they are in line with the tenets of *devotio moderna* as seen in such texts as Thomas à Kempis' *De imitatione Christi* (c. 1418).

1018   *thryve*. M: *prywe*, Eccles' emendation.

1024   *kyngys*. The texts of the *Novem Virtutes* read "knights" at this point, and, while "kyngys" could be an error for "knyghtys," it is also possible that the playwright changed the text deliberately since references to royalty are more important in *Wisdom* than references to mere nobility.

1043–45   *Upon thy nakyde feet and bare / Tyll the blode folwude . . . Ande aftyr eche stepe yt sene were.* Compare the bloody feet of the poor plowman's pitiable wife in "Piers the Plowman's Crede," line 436, as she walks barefoot across icy terrain; there the emotive force of the image provokes compassion in the audience.

1065, s.d.   The crowns which Anima, the Five Wits, and the three Mights now wear are more elaborate than the "chappelets" they wore at their first appearance.

1096–1107 In these lines, possibly the most extraordinary passage in the whole play, Wisdom (now explicitly equated with Christ) explains to Anima how his five senses, perfect in their lack of sin, are able to make atonement for her where her sinful senses fail. This explanation revolves around an emotional description of the pains which the crucifixion brought to each of Christ's senses, the images clearly drawn from the fifteenth-century devotional mode of affective piety, best exemplified by Nicholas Love's *Mirror of the Blessed Life of Jesus Christ.* Love explains the principle of imagining one's self in the place of Christ: "For to him that wolde serche the passion of oure lorde with alle his herte & alle his inwarde affeccione, there shuld come many deuout felynges & stirynges that he neuer supposede before. Of the whech he shuld fele a newe compassion & a newe loue, & haue newe gostly confortes, thorh the whech he shold perceyue him self turnede as it were in to a newe astate of soule, in the which astate thoo forseide gostly felynges, shold seme to him as a nerneste & partie of the blisse & joy to come" (p. 160).

1107   *dovehous*. The "dovehouse" image seems to have been traditional; Eccles gives examples of it in the *Ayenbite of Inwit*, the *Orologium*, Richard Rolle's *Meditiations on the Passion*, and *The Book of Margery Kempe*.

1108   *plesere*. M: *plesynge*, Eccles' emendation (for the rhyme with line 1106).

1123   Each of the Mights is returned to a state of grace through one of the theological virtues; Mind through "gostly felynge," that is faith, Understanding through hope (line 1127), and Will through love or charity (line 1135).

1137   This line is not in the manuscript, but there is no doubt that a line is missing from the stanza, and since the stanzas of the other three Mights and Anima each give a Latin couplet at this point, this would be the appropriate place for the missing line. The line immediately following in Colossians (3:9) does not fit, since it does not rhyme with "foly" in the next line; however, the line as quoted by Hilton in *Scale of Perfection*, Book 2, Chapter 31 does rhyme, and has been inserted here (following Eccles and Riggio). See Appendix 1.

1156   There is no change of speaker indicated in the manuscript at this point, though there is a line drawn across the page, which in almost all cases the scribe uses to indicate either a change of speaker or the beginning of a stage direction. Riggio has proposed that the scribe has drawn the usual line, but has forgotten to note the new speaker; she points out that it would be odd for Anima to offer the final blessing, noting that in the other Macro moralities the concluding benediction is given by "the figure representing divine authority: God the Father in [*The Castle of*] *Perseverance* and Mercy in *Mankind*" (*Play of Wisdom*, p. 307).

1159   *Our.* M: *on*, Eccles' emendation.

# APPENDIX 1: SOURCES

The following excerpts have been reedited for this volume unless otherwise noted. For full citations to complete editions of the extracted texts, see the bibliography.

THE PRIDE OF LIFE

The passage which clarifies the uncertain reading of line 347 appears frequently in both prose and verse texts of the fourteenth and fifteenth centuries; examples of both are given here. The *Gesta Romanorum* (Deeds of the Romans) was a very popular text which survives in a large number of manuscripts, and may well be the source for the line, though it appears frequently in lyrics of the period as well.

A. *GESTA ROMANORUM*, BRITISH LIBRARY MS ADDITIONAL 9066, fol. 54 (COMPARE *PRIDE OF LIFE*, LINE 347)

This is redde in the Cronycles of Rome that in the tyme of Antynyane the Emperour in the Citee of Rome befille [happened, befell] a grete pestilence of men and bestes and grete hungre in all the Empire. The comons risen agayn [against] her lordes and agayn her emperour.

The Emperour desired to wite [know] the cause of the tribulacions and diseases and, disposed hym forto putte a remedie agayn the forsaid disease, he called to hym foure wise Philisophers forto shew hym the cause of the grete vengeaunce.

Of the whiche philisophers the first said thus, "Gifte [reward, bribery] is domesman [judge] and gile [guile, deceit] is chapman [merchant], the grete hold no lawe, servantes have none awe."

The second said, "Witte [wit, skill, craft] is turned to trechery, and love into lechery. The holy day into Glotonye, and gentrie [gentility] into vilanye."

The third said, "Wise men are but scorned, and wedowes be sore yerned [harassed]; grete men are but glosed [flattered], and smale men born downe and mysloved [disliked, hated]."

The fourthe said, "Lordes wexen [become] blynde and kynnesmen ben unkynde; dethe out of mynde, and threwthe [truth] mayh no man fynde."

B. "THE ABUSES OF THE AGE," BRITISH LIBRARY MS HARLEY 2251, fol. 153r:

	Gift is made domesman,	*Reward (Bribery); judge*
	Gyle is made chapman,	*Guile; merchant*
	Lordes ben lawles,	
	And children ben awles.	*without awe or reverence*
5	Witte is torned to trechery,	*Wit (Skill, Craft)*
	Love is torened to lecher,	
	Pleye is torne to vilany,	*Sport (Play)*
	And haliday to gloteny.	
	Olde men ben skorned,	
10	Wymmen ben wowed.	*wooed (harassed)*
	Riche men ben pleasid,	
	And poremen ben diseasid.	*afflicted*
	Wise men ben blynde,	
	And kynrede is unkynde.	*kindred (family)*
15	The dede is out of mynde;	*death*
	Trew friende can noman fynde.	

WISDOM

The source material for the play which is printed here does not include the Bible, from which a number of passages derive. In particular, the opening conversation between Wisdom (Christ) and Anima relies heavily on the love-poetry of the Canticles, from which several direct quotations are taken.

A. THE *OROLOGIUM SAPIENTIAE*

The *Orologium Sapientiae* (Timekeeper of Wisdom) by the German mystic Heinrich Suso (c. 1295–1366) provided a substantial part of the first section of the play. The author did not use Heinrich's Latin text, but rather the anonymous English translation which was produced in the mid-fifteenth century under the title *The Sevene Poyntes of Trewe Love and Everlastynge Wisdame*. At least eight complete manuscripts of the English version survive, as well as five partial texts, and it was printed by William Caxton in 1491. The correspondence between the two texts is often very close; the playwright frequently preserves both the vocabulary and the sentence structure of the treatise. The passages printed here represent the closest correspondences between the two texts; a comparison of the play with its source is instructive from the point of view both of the author's use of the wording of the treatise as well as of his omissions. Also, many of the play's biblical quotations (both canonical and apocryphal) are taken directly from the English translation of Heinrich rather than from the Vulgate Bible or other standard sources. The text given here is taken from Oxford Bodleian Library, MS Douce 114, fols. 89v–148r.

(MS Douce 114, fols. 93r–94r; compare *Wisdom*, lines 1–79)

The maystere [teacher], everlastynge Wisdam, seyde, "First of the properté of the name and the love of everlastynge Wisdam, and how the discyple schalle have hym in felynge of that love bothe in beternesse and in swetnesse. First, if thou wolt wite [know] the properté and resone of my name, thou schalt understande that I am clepede [called] of hem that livene in erthe everlastynge Wisdam. The whiche name is most convenient and best acordynge to myne nobleye [nobility]. For thoughe hit so be that everye persone of the Holye Trinité taken by hit-selfe is Wisdam, and alle the persones to-gydere one everlastynge Wisdam, neverthelese, for als miche [much] as Wisdam is properlye applyede to the Sone and also hit falleth [pertains] to him by resone of his generacione [birth] specialye [especially], therefore the bylovede Sone of the Fadere is takene and understande in that manere significacione of Wisdame custumablye [usually], nowe as Godde and nowe as manne, nowe as he that is spouse of his Chirche and nowe as sche that is spouse and wyfe of everye chosene soule, that maye seye of everlastyng Wisdam in thees wordes of the Boke of Wisdam: "Hanc amavi et exquisivi a juventute mea et quesivi eam sponsam mi assumere, et amator factus sum forme illius." That is to seye, "She[1] I have loveded and I have utterlye souhte fro [from] myne youthe and I have desyrede for to have to mye spouse, and I am made a lovere of hir forme and schappe [appearance]." And also in the selfe [same] book thus, "Super salutem et omnem pulcritudinem dilexi sapienciam et proposui pro luce habere illam, venerunt mi omnia bona pariter cum illa." "Abovene heele [health] and alle bewté I have lovede Wisdam and I have purposede for to have hir as for mye lihte, and alle godes [good things] have comene to me with hir." Also of mye worthinesse hit is writen thus: "Sapiencia speciosior est sole et super omnem disposicionem stellarum luci comparata invenitur prior, candor est enim lucis eterne et speculum sine macula divine majestatis et ymago bonitatis illius." That is to seye, "Wisdam is feyrere thanne sonne and in comparisone of hir to liht she is foundene [found] passynge above alle the disposicione [display] of sterres, she is forsothe the bryhtnesse of everlastynge liht and the mirrour without of Goddes majesté and the ymage of his godenesse." Also thus: "Melior est sapiencia cuntis opibus preciosissimis et omne desiderabile non potest ei comparari, longitudo dierum in dextra ejus et in sinistra illius divicie et gloria." "Wisdam is bettur thanne alle manere of moste preciouse godes, and alle that may be desyreded may not be in comparisone lyke to hir; the lengh of yeres is in hire right syde and in hir lift [left] seyde richesses and joye."

And thus miche [much] touchygne the propreté and the worthenesse of mye name. But nowe, tochinge my love, beholde with a joyefulle mynde how hable I am to be lovede, howe lovelye to be clippede [embraced] and kyssede of a clene soule. O blessede is that soule to wham [whom] is grauntede in alle here lyfe, thouhe [though] it be but one tyme, to feele that hit be so. And thouh hit be so that deth falle [happen] therebye, hit schalle not be to him grevouse. For, sothelye, I am ever redye to him that lovethe me for to love ayenewarde [in return], and with him I am present in chirche and atte borde [meal], in the weye and in cloyster and in the market, so that there is no place but that there is present charité of Godde; for amonge alle othere spouses the goddelye Wisdam hath this sengulere [unique] propreté that sche may be present overalle to the desyre of hire lovere, and alle the sihynges [lamentations] for hire and desyres and all maner dedes and servyses sche as present

---

[1] The manuscript reads *sche this*. Perhaps the translator is attempting to indicate that the Latin demonstrative *hanc* is feminine.

knoweth anone. Also the sengulere prerogatyfe [advantage] of mye godenesse and love is so grete that, whoso tasteth therof thouh hit be but one lytele drope, aftere that he schalle halde alle the lustes and lykynges of the worlde but as dritte [dirt]. Mye love descharges [absolves] hem [them] that beth overleyde with the hevé birthene [burden] of sinnes, hit purifyeth and maketh clene the conscience, hit strengtheth the mynde and the soule, hit gevith fredam to hem that beth parfyte, and cowpleth [joins] and knitte hem [them] to here [their] everlastynge beginnynge. And what more — whoso taketh me into [as] his spouse and loveth me above alle thinge, he lyveth with tranquillyte and reste, he deeth [dies] with sykernesse [certainty (of salvation)], and in a manere he biginneth here the blisse and the joyes that schole [shall] laste ever worlde withoute ende.

We spekene manye thinges and yite [yet] we faylene [fail] in oure wordes, for the hye worthinesse of mye love there maye none tunge of menne ne of aungeles pleynlye telle; hit maye be in experience felt, but hit may not be fullye tolde or spokene, and therefore alle thees wordes of the makynge of goddelye love beth but as sodenlye rathere owt caste than in effecte plenerlye [more clearly] fulle spokene.

Thenne seyde the discyple to himselfe thus, "O Lorde Godde, howe manye gode thinges have[2] sovereynlye [supremely] fayre and worthi spouse! Why thanne makest thou dissimulacione or feynynge, whye assayest [test] not whether thou mayht have hire in to thi amyke [friend] or love? O, howe blessede were thou if thou mihteste wede [marry, wed] hir and have hir into [as] thi spouse! For thou art yonge and able to love, and ther maye none herte so clene be so solitarye by lakke of love. Wherefore nowe in fulle deliberacione I have utterlye sette that I schalle putte myeselfe to the deth, so that I maye hir gete in to amyke and spouse of me."

And thanne everlastynge Wisdam with a gladde and graciose chere [countenance] godelye salvede [greeted] hym and seyde schortlye [briefly] in thees wordes, "Fili, prebe mi cor tuum." "Sone, giffe me thi herte!"

(MS Douce 114, fols. 91r–92r; compare *Wisdom,* lines 100–04)

This passage appears somewhat earlier in the treatise than the previous one. Here, the Disciple describes the various schools of worldly wisdom in which he has previously studied prior to discovering the School of True Divinity, and the passage explains the — otherwise slightly odd — line in which Anima asks Wisdom to "Teche me the scolys of your dyvynyté" (line 100). The line can be understood approximately by taking "scolys" to mean "doctrines," but its background in this passage makes the author's choice of word much clearer. The passage also provides a direct source for lines 101–04.

There was sumtyme a devout discyple of Wisdam, the whiche aftere that in his youthe hadde gone to diverse scoles and lerede sere [many] sciences of mannus [man's] doctrine and worldlye wisdam, aftere he cam to more age and was towchede bye[3] to the trewe love of oure Lorde Jhesu, him thouhte miche [much] veyne [unprofitable] travayle [labor] in the forseyde sciences, wherefor he preyede continuelye and devoutlye to Godde, that he wolde not suffre him to departe from this lyfe til he cam to the knowelechyng and the kunynge [understanding] of sothefast [true] and sovereyne philosophye. And in the mene tyme as he

---

[2] The manuscript reads *here I spokene.*

[3] There may be a word missing in the text here; Horstmann suggests "desire."

went fro [from] studye to studye and fro scole to scole, sechynge bisilye that [that which] he desirede, but in none manere sothefastlye [truly] fyndynge but onelye as a ymage or a liknesse thereoffe, befelle upon a tyme, as he was in hees devoute meditaciones and preyeres, there aperede to his siht as hit were a wondere grete and large rounde hous like to the spere [sphere] of the firmamente, alle of brihte schinynge golde, sette alle aboute with fayre preciouse stones, in the whiche hous, that was departede [separated] in the middes, there were tweyn [two] mansiones, one above and anothere benethene [below], and eche of hem continede diverse doctours and maystres and wondere fele [many] disciples accordyng to hem. In the nethere [lower] mansione were maystres and discyples of alle naturele sciences and of alle craftes undere sonne, the wheche alle haddene [had] as hit were a manere [kind of] veyle upon here faces, and amonge the grete swinke [labor] and travayle that they haddene eche off heme [them] in his science and craft, thei were comfortede with a manere of swete drinke, the whiche quenchede not fullye here thriste; but hit, generynge [producing] a manere of dryenesse, made hem more thristlewe [thirsty] and more.

And whan the forseyde disciple hadde abedene [remained] a while in thoo [those] scoles and tastede of here drinke, his stomake overturnede and beganne to have a vomyte. Wherefore he laft thoo scoles and forsoke thees sciences, and went up to the seconde mansione, the whiche was wondere feyre and diverse-maner curioselye depeyntede [painted] and arayede [decorated]. And whanne he come thereto and stode before the dore, he fonde ther this manere superscripcione, "This is the scole of sothfaste [true] divinyté, where the maystresse [mistress] is everlastynge Wisdam, the doctrine is verité and trewth, and the ende everlastynge felicité." And whanne he hadde radde [read] this superscripcione, in alle hast he entrede in to that scole, coveitynge [desiring] with alle his inwarde desyre to be made a disciple of that scole, wherebye he hopede to come to that ende that he hadde longtyme desyrede.

But in this scole were thre ordres bothe of discyples and of doctours. Summe setene [sat] on the grounde bye the dore, the wheche lakkedene [lacked] trewe taste of divinyté and haddene here beholdynge [vision] and siht to [on] thoo [those] thinges that were without-forthe [external]. Thei that were of the secounde ordre, profytede not ferventlye, but in a manere semede [seemed] as thei stodene stille. But thei that were of the thridde ordre, setene [sat] nihe [near] the maystre and thei, drinkynge the water of helefulle [healthful, tending towards salvation] Wisdam that came out of his mouthe, thei were made so drunkene that thei foryetene [forgot] hemselfe [themselves] and alle othere worldlye thinges, havynge here [their] hertes and here eyene [eyes] ever upwarde to the mayster and ferventlye ravischede in to his love and hevenelye thinges.

And whenne the discyple hadde bisilye [carefully] beholdene thees thinges, he was gretlye awondrede, and namelye of that thinge that in one scole and of one sothfastnesse [truth] ther was so grete diversité and unliknesse in manye maystres and disciples. And thanne he herde, as him thouhte [it seemed to him], a voyce, spekynge to him in thes manere wordes, "Thoo [Those] thre ordres that thou hast seene, beth thre manere of studiyng and techynge holye writte [scripture]. The first manere is fleschelye, and that havene thei that bene copiose and habundant in the letterere [lettered] science [knowledge] without the spiryte, the wheche the more kunynge [understanding] that thei bene, the more thei bene blowne [inflated] and fillede with pryde, and bene noyes [harmful] both to hemselfe and to othere, the wheche sekene not in here kunynge [knowledge] Goddes wirchepe and lovynge or to soule-hele [salvation] and edificacione of hemselfe and othere, but thei bisiyne [concern] hem [them] onelye about here owne worldlye promocione [advancement]. The secounde manere of lerenynge and techynge holye writ is bestelye [brutishly], and that is in hem that in scole-excersyse in a symple manere sechene thoo thinges that bene nedefulle to soule-hele, but thei beth necligente and slowe to profyte in the fervour of charité and love to Godde and hevenelye thinges. The thridde manere is spirituele and gostlye, and that is in hem that with alle here mihtes and hertlye affecciones travayle [labor] and bysyene [busy] hem to gete thoo thinges that longene [belong] to perfeccione, so that, as here understand-ynge profyteth in kunynge [understanding], so here [their] soule and here affeccione be fillede with the Wisdam of Godde, the wheche tastene and beholdene the swetnesse of oure Lorde, and be [by] here kunynge of holye write techene and ledene hemselfe and othere in to blessede ende."

Wherefore the forseyde discyple, levynge alle the tothere [others], soverenlye [particu-larly] desyrede to have his abidynge and dwellynge with hem, and offrede him to be with hem [them] a trewe discyple of that hevenelye maystre, everlastynge Wisdam. And so he, neyhinge [drawing near] to the mayster, beganne to speke to him in this manere, "O thou sovereyne and everlastynge Wisdam, sithene hit is so that alle menne by kynde [nature] de-syrene [desire] for to have kunynge, and in thee, universele prynce and auctor [creator] of kynde, alle manere tresores of wisdam and kunynge beth hidde, and also thou art makere of alle thinge and hast alle manere of science and alle thinge thou seest and knowest. Therefore I aske of thee with a gredye [greedy] desyre of alle mye hert that thou opune to me the tresoreye of thi sovereyn Wisdam, and that compendioslye [thoroughly] and in schorte [brief] wordes, for thei that nowe bethe lovene and haveth likynge in schorte speche, and of makynge bokes is none ende — alle the worlde is fillede with dyverse doctrines, and there beth a twosende [thousand] manere of livynge: one liveth in this manere and anothere in that manere. Ther beth so manye bokes and tretees [treatises] of vyces and vertues and of dyverse doctrynes, that this schort lyve schalle rathere have an ende of anye manne thanne he maye owthere studye hem or rede hem. Wherefore, thou everlastynge sovereyne Wisdam, I desyre and aske of thee that thou teche me in schort manere that hevenelye divinité, the whiche without errour standeth in thi Wisdam and in trewe love of thee, blessede Jhesu."

The mayster, everlastynge Wisdam, answerede thus, "Mye dere sone, wille thou noht savere [take pleasure] in kunynge to hye [too much], but drede [beware]! Here me nowe and I schalle teche the thinges that beth [will be] profitable to thee. I schall give thee a chosen gifte, for myne doctryne schalle be thi lyfe. Wherefore, takynge oure biginnynge of helefulle [healthy, tending toward salvation] disciplyne at the drede of Godde, the wheche is the be-ginnynge of Wisdam, I shalle teche thee by order seven poyntes of mye love, whereinne stant [stands] soverene Wisdam and the perfeccion of alle gode and rihtwis [righteous] lyvynge in this worlde."

B. WALTER HILTON'S *THE SCALE OF PERFECTION*[4]

The fourteenth-century mystic Walter Hilton (c. 1330–1396) studied law, probably at Cam-bridge, before entering the priesthood and becoming an Augustinian canon at the abbey of Thurgarton, Nottinghamshire, where he is likely to have become head of the abbey. His

---

[4] Excerpted from Thomas H. Bestul's edition (2000).

spiritual treatise *The Scale of Perfection* is a comprehensive manual for living a holy life, focusing in particular on the idea that the soul must be purified of all sin before union with God is possible. Although addressed to a Carthusian recluse, it became one of the most popular works of devotional literature in English before the Reformation of the sixteenth century.

Book 2, Chapter 1 (compare *Wisdom,* lines 103–06)
And in the bigynnynge, yif [if] thou wole [will] witen [know] pleynli what I mene bi this image, I telle thee forsothe [in truth] that y undirstonde not ellis but thyn owen soule; for thi soule and my soule and everi resonable soule is an image, and that a worthi image, for it is the ymage of God, as the apostel seith: *Vir est ymago dei* (1 Corinthians 11:7). That is, man is the image of God and maad to the image and to the liknesse of Him, not in bodili schap [form] withoutin, but in the myghtes [powers] of it withinne, as Holi Writ seith: *Formavit deus hominem ad similitudinem suam* (Genesis 1:27). That is, oure Lord God schoop [formed] in soule man to the ymage and the liknesse of Him. This is the ymage that I have spoke of and schal speken of. This ymage, maad to the liknesse of God in the first schap-ynge [forming] was wondirli [wonderfully] faire and bright, fulle of brennynge [burning] love and goostli [spiritual] light. But thorugh synne of the first man Adam it was disfigured and forschapen [deformed] into anothir liknesse . . .

Book 2, Chapter 2 (compare *Wisdom,* lines 109–24)
Now is it sooth [true] mankynde, that was hool [whole] in Adam the first man, trespaced agens [against] God so wondir grevousli whanne hit forfetide the special biddynge [com-mand] of God and consentide to the fals conceile [counsel] of the feend [devil], that it deservide rightwiseli [justly] for to have be departid [separated] from Him and dampned to helle withouten ende — so fer forth [to the extent], that stondinge the rightwisenesse of God [were the righteousness of God to stand], the trespaas myght not be forgeven but yif [unless] amendis and ful satisfaccioun were first maad therfore. But this amendes myght no man make that was man oonli and come out of Adam by kyndeli [natural] generacion, for this skile [reason], for the trespas and the unworschipe [dishonor] was endeles gret, and therfore it passide [surpassed] mannys myght [power] for to make amendis for it. And also for this skile: he that hath trespaced and schal make amendis, hym bihoveth gyve [it is necessary for him to give] to hym that he trespacide unto al that he oweth though that he hadde not tres-paced, and also over [beyond] that, hym bihoveth gyve him sumwhat [something] that he oweth not, but oonli [only because] for that he trespacid. But oonly mankynde hadde not [nought] wherwith he myght paie God for his trespaas, over that he ought [owed] Hym. For what good dede that man myght doon in bodi or in soule, it was but his dette. For everi man oweth [is obliged], as the Gospel seith, for to love God with al his herte and al his soule and alle his myghtes; and betere myght he not doo than this. And nevertheleees this deede suf-ficed not to the reformynge of mankynde, ne [nor] this myght not he doon but yif he hadde first be reformed. Than nedid it [it was necessary] that yif mannys soule schulde be reformed and the trespaas maad good, that oure Lord God Hymsilf schulde reforme this image and make amendis for this trespaas, syn [since] that no man myght. But that myght He not doo in His Godhede, for He myght not, ne ought not, make amendis bi suffrynge of peyne in His owen kynde [nature]. Therfore it nedide that He schulde take the same mankynde that hadd trespaced, and bicome man; and that myght He not by the comon lawe of kyndeli [natural] generacion, for it was impossibile Goddis sone to be born of a touchid [touched (sexually)] woman. Therfore He moste bicome man thorugh a gracious [i.e., through grace]

generacioun, bi wirkynge of the Holi Goost, of a clene [pure] gracious maiden, oure Ladi Seynt Marie. And so was it doon. For oure Lord Jhesu Crist, Goddis sone, bicam man, and thorough His precious deeth that He suffride made amendis to the Fadir of hevene for mannys [man's] gilt. And that myght He wel doon, for He was God, and He oughte [owed] not for Hymsilf, but for as mykil as He was man born of the same kynde that Adam was that first trespacede. And so, though He ought not for His owen persone, for Himsilf myght not synne, neverthelees He ought it of His free wille for the trespas of mankynde, the whiche kynde He took for savacioun [salvation] of man of His endeles merci. For sooth [truth] it is ther was nevere man that myght yelde to God onythinge of his owene that he ought not, but oonli this blissid man Jhesu Crist. For He myght paien [pay] thingis that He oughte not as for Hymsilf, and that was not but o [one] thynge: and that was for to gyve His preciouse liyf [life] by wilfull takynge of deeth for love of sothfastnesse [truth]. This ought He nout [owed He not]. As mykil good as He myght doo to the worschipe [honor] of God in His liyf, was al but dette. But for to take deeth for love of ryghtwisenesse [righteousness], He was not bounden therto. He was bounde to rightfulnesse, but He was not bounden to dyen. For deeth is oonli a peyne [punishment] ordeyned of God to man for his owen synne; but oure Lorde Jhesu synned nevere, ne He myght not synnen, and therefore He oughte [was obliged] nought for to dien. And yit wilfulli He diede, than paid He to God more thanne He oughte [owed]. And syn [since] that was the beste manere [kind of] deede and most worthi that evere was doon, therfore was it resonable that the synne of mankynde schulde be forgyven, in as mykil [much] as mankynde had founden a man of the same kynde withoutin weem [blemish] of synne, that is Jhesu, that myght make amendis for the trespaas doon and myght paien oure Lord God al that he oughte, and overmore [moreover], that he oughte not. Thanne siththe [since] oure Lord Jhesu, God and man, diede thus for savacion of mannys soule, it was rightful that synne schulde be forgyven and mannys soule, that was His image, schulde mow be [be able to be] reformyd and restorid to the first likenesse and to the blisse of hevene.

Book 2, Chapter 6 (compare *Wisdom*, lines 125–30)
Two maner of synne maken a soule to lese the schap [image] and the liknesse of God. That oon is callid original, that is the first synne. That othir is callid actuel [actual, i.e., sins actively committed, as opposed to inherited original sin] synne, that is wilfulli doon. Thise two synnes putten a soule fro the blisse of hevene and dampnen it to the eendeles pyne [pain] of helle, but yif it be thorugh grace of God reformed to His liknesse, or [before] it passe hens out of this lif. Nevertheles, two remedies there aren agens thise two synnes, bi the whiche a forschapen [deformed] soule mai be restored ageyn. Oon is the sacrament of baptym [baptism] agens the orignal synne; anothir is the sacrament of penaunce agens the actuel synne. The soule of a childe that is born and is uncristened, bicause of the orignal synne hath no liknesse of God; he is not [nothing, naught] but an image of the feend and a brond [firebrand] of helle. But as soone as it is cristened, it is reformed to the ymage of God, and thorugh vertu of feith of Holi Chirche sodeynli is turned fro the liknes of the feend and maad like to an angel of hevene.

Book 2, Chapter 13 (compare *Wisdom*, lines 133–48)
For thou schalt undirstonde that a soule hath two parties. The toon is called the sensualité; that is the fleschli feelynge bi the fyve outeward wittes [senses], the whiche is comoun to man and to beest. Up [Of] the whiche sensualité, whanne it is unskilfulli [irrationally] and unor-

dynateli [improperly] rulid, is maad the image of synne, as I have bifore seid, for than is the sensualité synne, whanne it is not rulid aftir resoun. That tothir [other] partie is callid reson, and that is departid [divided] on two — the overe [upper] partie and the nethere [lower] partie. The overe is likned to a man, for it schulde be maister and sovereyne, and that is propirli the ymage of God, for bi that oonli the soule knoweth God and loveth God. And the nethere is likned to a woman, for it schulde be buxum [obedient] to the overe partie of resoun, as a woman is buxum to man. And that liyth in knowynge and rulynge of ertheli thinges, for to use hem discreteli aftir nede and for to refuse hem whanne it is no nede; and for to have ai [always] with it thyn iye [eye] upward to the overe partie of resoun, with drede and with reverence for to folwe it.

Book 2, Chapter 12 (compare *Wisdom,* lines 148–70)
Fair is mannys soule, and foule is a mannys soule. Fair in as mykil [much] as it is reformed in trouthe to the liknesse of God, but it is foule in as mykil as it is yit medelid [mingled, mixed] with fleschli felynges and unskilful [irrational] stirynges of this ymage of synne. Foule withouten as it were a beest, faire withinne like to an angel. Foule in feelynge of the sensualité, fair in trouthe of the resoun. Foule for the fleschli appetite, faire for the good wil. Thus fair and thus foule is a chosen soule, seiynge Holi Writ thus: *Nigra sum, sed formosa, filie Ierusalem sicut tabernacula Cedar et sicut pelles Salomonis* (Canticles 1:4). I am blak, but I am fair and schapli, yee doughteris of Jerusalem, as the tabernaculis of Cedar and as the skynnes of Salomoun. That is: Yee angelis of hevene, that aren doughteres of the highe Jerusalem, wondreth not on me, ne dispice [despise] me not for my blak schadwe, for though I be blak withoute bicause of my fleschli kynde, as is a tabernacle of Cedar, nevertheles I am ful fair withinne as is the skyn of Salomon, for y am reformed to the likenesse of God. Bi Cedar is undirstonde myrkenesse [darkness], and that is the devyl. Bi tabernacle of Cedar is undir-stonde a reprevid [condemned] soule, the whiche is a tabernacule of the devyl. Bi Salomon, that bitokeneth peseble [peaceable], is undirstonden oure Lord, for He is pees and pesible. Bi the skyn of Salomon is undirstonden a blissid aungel, in whom oure Lord woneth [dwells] and is hid, as lif is hid withinne the skyn of a quyk [living] bodi, and therfore is an angel likened to a skyn.

Thanne mai a chosen soule with meke trust in God and gladnesse in herte seie thus: Though I be blak bicause of my bodi of synne, as is a reprevid [condemned] soule that is the tabernacle of the feend, neverthelees I am withinne wel faire thorugh trouthe and good wille, like to an angil of hevene. For so seith he in anothir place: *Nolite considerare me quia fusca sum, quoniam decoloravit me sol* (Canticles 1:5). That is: Biholdeth me not for y am swart [dark], for the sunne hath defaded me. The sunne maketh a skyn swart onli withoute and not withinne, and it bitokeneth this fleschli liyf. Therfore seith a chosen soule thus: "Repreve me not for y am swart, for the swartenesse that y have is al withouten, of touchynge and of berynge this ymage of synne. But it is nothinge withinne." And therfore soothli, though it be so that a chosen soule reformed in feithe dwelle in this bodi of synne, and feele the same fleischli stirynges and use the same bodili werkes as doth a tabernacle of cedar, so fer forth [to the extent] that in mannes dome [judgment] ther schulde no difference be bitwixe that oon and that tothir — neverthelees withinne in here soules is there ful grete diversité, and in the sight of God is there ful grete twynnynge [separation].

Book 1, Chapter 12 (compare *Wisdom,* line 231)
The knyttyng and the festenynge of Jhesu to a mannys soule is bi good wille and a greet
desire to Hym oonli, for to love and for to have Hym and see Him in His blisse.

Book 2, Chapter 31 (compare *Wisdom,* lines 1122–45)
For now bi the grace of oure Lord Jhesu schal y speke a litil as me thenketh more openli of
reformynge in feelynge — what it is and how it is maad, and whiche aren goostli feelynges
that a soule receyveth.

   Neverthelees first, that thou take not this maner of spekynge of reformynge of a soule
in feelynge as feynynge or fantasie, therfore I schal grounden it in Seynt Poules wordis,
where he seith thus: *Nolite conformari huic seculo, sed reformamini in novitate sensus vestri* (Romans 12:2). That is: Ye that aren thorough grace reformed in feith, conforme yow not
henneforward [henceforth] to maneres of the world, in pride, in covetise, and in othere
synnes; but be ye reformed in newehede [newness] of youre feelynge. Loo, heere thou maist
see that Seynt Poul speketh of reformynge in feelynge; and what that newe feelynge is he
expounneth in anothir place thus: *Ut impleamini in agnicione voluntatis eius, in omni intellectu
et sapiencia spirituali* (Colossians 1:9). That is: We praien God that ye mowen [may] ben
fulfilled in knowynge of Goddis wille, in al undirstondyng and in al maner goostli wisdom;
that is, in reformynge in feelynge. For thou schalt undirstonde that the soule hath two
manere of feelynges: on withoute of the fyve bodili wittes, anothir withinne of the goostli
wittes, the whiche aren propirli the myghtis of the soule, mynde, reson, and wille. Whanne
thorough grace thise myghtes aren fulfilled in al undirstondinge of the wille of God and in
goostli wisdom, than hath the soule newe gracious feelynges. That this is sooth, he schewith
in anothir place thus: *Renovamini spiritu mentis vestre, et induite novum hominem, qui secundum
deum creatus est in iusticia, sanctitate, et in veritate* (Ephesians 4:23–24). Be yee now renued in
the spirit of youre soule; that is, ye schullen ben reformed not in bodili feelynge ne in
imaginacion, but in the overe partie [upper part] of youre resoun. And clothe yow in a newe
man, that is schapen aftir God in rightwisenesse, holinesse, and soothfastnesse. That is, your
reson, that is propirli the ymage of God thorough grace of the Holi Goost, schal be clothid
in a newe light of soothfastenesse [truth], holynesse, and rightwisenesse [righteousness] and
thanne is it reformed in feelynge. For whanne the soule hath perfight [perfect] knowynge
of God, than is it reformed. Thus seith Seynt Poul: *Exspoliantes veterem hominem cum actibus
suis; induite novum, qui renovatur in agnicione dei, secundum ymaginem eius qui creavit eum*
(Colossians 3:9–10). Spoile [Despoil] yousilf of the oolde man with alle his deedis; that is,
casteth fro yow the love of the world with alle wordli maneris. And clothe you in a newe
man; that is, ye schullen be renewed in the knowynge of God aftir the liknesse of Hym that
made yow.

Book 2, Chapter 9 (compare *Wisdom,* lines 1154–60*)*
Of this reformynge in feith spekith Seynt Poul thus: *Justus autem ex fide vivit* (Hebrews
10:38). The rightwise [righteous] man lyveth in feith. That is, he that is maad rightful [just]
bi baptym or penaunce, he lyveth in feith, the whiche sufficeth to savacion and to heveneli
pees, as Seynt Poul seith: *Justificati ex fide, pacem habemus ad deum* (Romans 6:1). This is, we
that aren righted [justified] and reformed thorough feith in Crist han pees and acord maad
atwixe God and us, not agenstondynge [withstanding] the vicious feelinges of oure bodi of
synne.

Book 2, Chapter 26 (compare *Wisdom*, lines 1160–64)
Thus seith Hooli Writ: *Vobis qui timetis domini orietur sol iusticie* (Malachi 4:2). The trewe sunne of rightwisenesse [righteousness], that is, oure Lord Jhesu, schal springe to yow that dreden Him; that is, to meke [meek] soulis that meke [humble] hemself undir her even Cristene [fellow Christians] bi knowynge of here [their] owen wrecchidnesse, and casten hemsilf doun undir God bi noghtynge [rendering as nothing] of hemsilf in here owen substaunce thorugh reverente drede and goostli biholding of Him lastandli [constantly], for that is perfight [perfect] mekenesse.

C. WALTER HILTON'S *EPISTLE ON THE MIXED LIFE* (VERNON MS TEXT, fols. 353v, COL. 1–356, COL. 2)[5]

Hilton rejected the idea that the life closest to God was that of the cloistered monk or hermit, supporting instead the notion that the best life is a "mixed" life devoted to service and prayer in the world rather than withdrawal from it. Lucifer's arguments in favor of the mixed life, intended to draw Mind, Will, and Understanding away from a monastic existence, are largely drawn from Hilton's discussion, although based on a very superficial reading of it.

Chapter 27 (fol. 356r, col. 1; compare *Wisdom*, lines 401–29)
And I halde [maintain] that hit is good to thee for to use this maner in what devocion that thou be, that thou hange [remain] not longe ther-upon, outhur [either] for to putte fro [from] thee thi mete [food] or thi slepe in tyme, or for to [di]sese [harm] any othur man unskilfuli [unreasonably]. *Omnia tempus habent:* Al thing hath tyme (Ecclesiates 3:1)..

Chapter 1 (fol. 353v, col. 2)
Thou schalt not utturli [entirely] folwe thi desyre for to leve [abandon] ocupacions & bisynes of the world whuch are nedeful to use in rulyng of thi sel[f] & of al othur that are under thi keping, & geve thee hol[i] [entirely] to gostly [spiritual] occupacion in preyers & meditacions as hit were a monk or a frere [friar] or eny othur mon that were not bounde to the world be [by] children & servauns as thou art: for hit falleth [is appropriate] not to thee; yif [if] thou do so, thou kepest not the ordre of charité. Also, yif thou woldest utterli leve gostli occupacion, nomeli [that is] aftur the grace that God hath geven to thee, & sette thee holliche [entirely] to bisynes of the world, to fulfillyng of actif lyf, as fully as anothur that never feled devocion, thou leosest [will lose] the ordre of charité, for thi stat [estate] asketh for to do bothe, in diverse tymes.

Chapter 2 (fol. 353v, col. 2)
Thou schalt medle [mix] the werkes of actif lyf with gostly werkes of contemplatyf lyf, and then dost thou wel. For thou schalt o [one] tyme with Martha be bisy for to ruile & governe thin houshold, thi children, thi servauns, thi neighebors, and thi tenauntes. Yif [If] thei do wel, cumforte hem therin & help hem; yif thei don uvel [evil], tech hem to amende hem & chastise hem. And thou [schalt] also loke & knowe wysli that thi thinges & thi worldly godes be [by] rightli kept be thi servauntes, governed & trewely dispendet [spent], that thou might

---

[5] Transcribed from the manuscript.

the more plenteuousli with hem fulfille the dedes of merci to thin evencristen [fellow Christians]. A nothur tyme thou schalt with Marie leve the bisynes of the world & sitte doun at the feet of ur Lord be mekenes in preyers & holy thoughtes & in contemplacion of him as he geveth thee grace.

Chapter 5 (fol. 354r, cols. 1–2)
Oure Lord for to stere [direct] sum men to use this medled [mixed] lyf, tok upon him self the persones of such maner of men, bothe of prelates & curates of holy chirche & of othur such as are disposed as I have seid, and gaf to hem ensaumple [example] be his owne worchyng [deeds] that thei schulde use this medled lyf as he dude [did]. O [One] tyme he comuned [communed] & medled [mixed] with men, schewyng to hem his dedes [of] merci, for he taught the unkonnyng [uneducated] by his preching, he visyted the seke & heled hem of heor [their] sores, he fedde the hungri & cumforted hem that were sori [grieving]. Anothur tyme he lafte [left] the conversacion of al worldly men & of his disciples also & went alone in to desert upon the hulles [hills] & contyn[u]ed al the night in preyers as the gospel seith. This medled lyf schewed ur Lord in him self to ensaumple of hem that han [have] take the staat [condition] & the charge of this medled lyf, that thei schulde o [one] tyme geve hem to bisynes of worldly thynges in resonable nede, & to werkes of actyf lyf in profyt of heor [their] evencristne [fellow Christians] whuch thei have cure [care] of; anothur tyme geve hem hol[i] [entirely] to contemplacion be devocion in preyer & in meditacion . . . .

D. (ST. BERNARD?), *MEDITATIONES PIISSIME DE COGNITIONE HUMANAE CONDITIONIS*, MIGNE, *PL* 184R, COLS. 485A–487C (COMPARE *WISDOM*, LINES 95–98, 177–90, 245–82)

The *Meditationes* are probably not by St. Bernard, although most medieval manuscripts of the text attribute it to him; the work provides the principal source for the idea that the earthly powers of the soul form a trinity: Mind, Will, and Understanding or, as the treatise phrases it, "memoria," "intelligencia," and "voluntas." The work's popularity is attested both by its extensive use by Pietro Alighieri, Dante's son, in his commentary on the *Paradiso* dating from about 1340, as well as by the publication of an English translation in 1496 by Wynkyn de Worde, *The Medytacyens of Saynt Bernarde*. Both the Latin text and English translation are included here, since it is likely that the author was working from the Latin text.

1. Multi multa sciunt, et se ipsos nesciunt. Alios inspiciunt, et se ipsos deserunt. Deum quaerunt per ista exteriora, deserentes sua interiora, quibus interior est Deus. Idcirco ab exterioribus redeam ad interiora, et ab inferioribus ad superiora ascendam: ut possim cognoscere unde venio, aut quo vado; quid sum, vel unde sum; et ita per cognitionem mei valeam pervenire ad cognitionem Dei. Quanto namque in cognitione mei proficio, tanto ad cognitionem Dei accedo. Secundum interiorem hominem tria in mente mea invenio, per quae Deum recolo, conspicio, et concupisco. Sunt autem haec tria, memoria, intelligentia, voluntas sive amor. Per memoriam reminiscor: per intelligentiam intueor; per voluntatem amplector. Cum Dei reminiscor, in memoria mea eum invenio, et in ea de eo et in eo delector, secundum quod ipse mihi donare dignatur. Intelligentia intueor quid sit Deus in se ipso; quid in Angelis, quid in sanctis, quid in creaturis, quid in hominibus. In se ipso est incomprehensibilis, quia principium et finis: principium sine principio, finis sine fine. Ex me intelligo quam incomprehensibilis sit Deus; quoniam me ipsum intelligere non possum,

quem ipse fecit. In Angelis est desiderabilis, quia in eum desiderant prospicere: in sanctis est delectabilis, quia in eo assidue felices laetantur: in creaturis est admirabilis, quia omnia potenter creat, sapienter gubernat, benigne dispensat: in hominibus est amabilis, quia eorum Deus est, et ipsi sunt populus ejus. Ipse in eis habitat tanquam in templo suo, et ipsi sunt templum ejus: non dedignatur singulos, neque universos. Quisquis ejus meminit, eumque intelligit ac diligit, cum illo est.

2. Diligere eum debemus, quoniam ipse prior dilexit nos, et ad imaginem et similitudinem suam nos fecit, quod nulli alii creaturae donare voluit. Ad imaginem Dei facti sumus; hoc est, ad intellectum et notitiam Filii, per quem intelligimus et cognoscimus Patrem, et accessum habemus ad eum. Tanta cognatio est inter nos et Dei Filium, quod ipse imago Dei est, et nos ad imaginem ejus facti sumus; quam cognationem etiam ipsa similitudo testatur, quoniam non solum ad imaginem, sed et ad similitudinem ejus facti sumus. Oportet itaque id quod ad imaginem est, cum imagine convenire, et non in vacuum nomen imaginis participare. Repraesentemus ergo in nobis imaginem ejus in appetitu pacis, in intuitu veritatis, et in amore charitatis. Teneamus eum in memoria, portemus in conscientia, et ubique praesentem veneremur. Mens siquidem nostra eo ipso ejus imago est, quo ejus capax est, ejusque particeps esse potest. Non propterea ejus imago est, quia sui meminit mens, seque intelligit ac diligit; sed quia potest meminisse, intelligere, ac diligere a quo facta est: quod cum facit, sapiens ipsa fit. Nihil enim tam simile est illi summae Sapientiae, quam mens rationalis, quae per memoriam, intelligentiam et voluntatem in illa Trinitate ineffabili consistit. Consistere autem in illa non potest, nisi ejus meminerit, eumque intelligat, ac diligat. Meminerit itaque Dei, ad cujus imaginem facta est; eumque intelligat, diligat, atque colat, cum quo potest semper esse beata. Beata anima, apud quam Deus requiem invenit, et in cujus tabernaculo requiescit. Beata quae dicere potest: *Et qui creavit me, requievit in tabernaculo meo* (Ecclesiastes 24:12). Negare siquidem requiem coeli ei non poterit.

3. Cur ergo nos deserimus, et in his exterioribus Deum quaerimus, qui apud nos est, si nos velimus esse apud eum? Revera nobiscum est, et in nobis: sed adhuc per fidem, donec videre mereamur per speciem. *Novimus*, inquit Apostolus, *habitare Christum per fidem in cordibus nostris* (Ephesians 3:17): quia Christus in fide, fides in mente, mens in corde, cor in pectore. Per fidem ergo recolo Deum creatorem; adoro redemptorem, exspecto salvatorem. Credo videre in omnibus creaturis, habere in me ipso; et, quod his omnibus ineffabiliter jucundius atque beatius est, cognoscere in se ipso. Patrem namque et Filium cum sancto Spiritu cognoscere, vita est aeterna, beatitudo perfecta, summa voluptas. Oculus non vidit, nec auris audivit, nec in cor hominis ascendit, quanta claritas, quanta suavitas, et quanta jucunditas maneat nos in illa visione, quando Deum facie ad faciem videbimus; qui est lux illuminatorum, requies exercitatorum, patria redeuntium, vita viventium, corona vincentium. Ita in mente mea quamdam imaginem illius summae Trinitatis invenio: ad quam summam Trinitatem recolendam, inspiciendam, et diligendam, ut ejus recorder, ea delecter, et eam complectar et contempler, totum id quod vivo, debeo referre. Mens imago Dei est, in qua sunt haec tria: id est memoria, intelligentia et voluntas. Memoriae attribuimus omne quod scimus, etiamsi non inde cogitemus. Intelligentiae tribuimus omne quod verum cogitando invenimus, quod etiam memoriae commendamus: voluntati, omne quod cognitum et intellectum, bonum et verum esse expetimus. Per memoriam Patri similes sumus, per intelligentiam Filio, per voluntatem Spiritui sancto. Nihil in nobis tam simile Spiritui sancto est, quam voluntas vel amor sive dilectio, quae excellentior voluntas est.

Dilectio namque donum Dei est, ita quod nullum hoc dono Dei est excellentius. Dilectio namque quae ex Deo est, et Deus est, proprie Spiritus sanctus dicitur, per quam charitas Dei diffusa est in cordibus nostris (Romans 5:5), per quam tota Trinitas in nobis habitat.

The English version is printed from Wynkyn de Worde's version, printed in 1496 (STC: 1917; sig. Bi, Aiii). A few minor printer's errors have been silently corrected.

How man by knowledge & understondynge of hymselfe maye knowe God, and how the soule of man is the ymage of God.

1. Many there ben that know & understonde many other thynges, & yet they knowe not theyr owne selfe. They take moche hede [pay much attention] to other, but they loke not well to themselfe. They leve theyre inwarde & goostly thynges, and seke God amonge outwarde thynges, the whyche is within theym. Therfore I shall come fro [from] those thynges that ben [are] outwarde to inwarde thynges, & from inwarde thynges I shall lyft my mynde to thynges above, that I may knowe wherof I came, and whether I go, what I am, and wherof I am. And so by knowlege of myself, I may ascende & come to the knowlege of God, for the more I proyffyte in knowlege of my self, the more nygh [near] I drawe to the knowlege of God.

On the inward mannys behalfe I fynde thre thynges in my soul wherby I remembre, beholde & desyre my lorde God. The whiche ben, the mynde, the understondynge, & wyl or love. By the mynde I remembre Him; by the understondynge I beholde Him goostly [spiritually]; and by wyll or love I love and desyre Him. Whan I remember God I fynde in Hym in my mynde, & fele therin in Him swetnesse & plesyre of Hym, lyke as he vouchesaufe [grants] to gyve me. By the understondynge I beholde in Hym what He is in Hymself, what in holy angellys, and what in His blessyd sayntes, what in His creatures, & what in mankynde. In Hymselfe He is incomprehensyble for He is both begynnynge & ende: Begynnynge without begynnynge, & ende wythout ende. By myself I understonde how He is comprehensyble whan I may not atteyne to understondynge and knowlege of my self whome He hath made. In holy angellys He is plesaunt and desyderable [desireable], for theyre desyre is alwaye to beholde Hym. In sayntes He is delectable, for they happy & blessyd delyte them in Hym contynually. In creatures He is mervelous, for by his myghte & power He createth all thynges the whiche He governeth moost wysely, & dystrybutyth moost benyngnely: In mankynde He is amyable & lovely, for He is theyr God & they ben His people. And He dwelleth with theym as in His owne temple and they ben the temple of Hym. Who somever [Whoever] hath mynde and thynketh on Him, understondeth Him and loveth Hym, He is with hym.

2. Sothely [truly] we owe [ought] to love Hym moche, syth [since] He hath loved us soo moche & made us after His owne ymage & lyknes & soo hath He done to none [no other] erthly creature. Sothely it behoveth [is appropriate] that the thynge that is made after an ymage to be accordynge and lyke to the ymage or symylytude that it is fourmed after, and not to have unworthely the name of an ymage in vayne. Therfore lete us shewe in us thymage [the image] of Hym in desyrynge of peas and regardynge of trouth. Lete us holde and kepe Hym by perfyte love and charyté in our mynde. Let us bere Him in our conscyence and to Hym presente in every place lete us do due reverence and worshyppe.

Our soul sothly is the ymage of God, for asmoche as it is apte and mete to take and receyve Hym and maye [perhaps] be partener of Hym. It is the ymage of Hym, not only that it remembreth itselfe, understondyth or loveth itselfe, but by cause it maye remembre, understonde, and love Hym. whiche made it. And whan it soo dooth, thenne is it wyse, for sothly there is no thynge more lyke to the hyghe wysdome of almyghty God, than is a resonable soule, whyche by mynde, understondynge and love resteth in the blessyd Trynyte. In whiche she [i.e., the soul] maye not reste and abyde, but yf she remembre Hym, understonde and also love Hym.

But yf she thynke dylygently on her lorde God, after thymage of Whome she is created and made. And understonde, love, honoure, and worshyppe Hym wyth Whome she maye eternally abyde and reste in perfyghte Joye and blysse. Sothly that soule is ryghte happy and blessyd in whome oure Lorde fyndeth restynge, and in whoos tabernacle He dwelleth and resteth. That is an happy soule that maye saye, "My Lorde & maker hath restyd in my tabernacle." Soothly He shal not deny to such a soule the everlastynge reste of heven.

3. O, why thenne loke we not in our self, but seke [seek] our Lorde amonge outwarde thynges, the whyche is with us yf we wyll be with Him? Sothly He is both with us and in us,[6] but that as yet is by fayth, unto suche tyme as we maye deserve to see Him clerly. "We knowe," sayth the apostle, "that by fayth Cryste abydeth in our hertes." By fayth I remembre my maker, I worshyp my mercyfull redemer, and abyde [await] my savyoure. I byleve that He lyveth in all creatures, that He dwelleth within me. And also I truste to knowe Him in Himself, the whiche is moche more blyssfull & Joyfull than all thyse ben [are], for sothly to knowe perfytely the Fader, the Sone, & the Holy Goste in everlastynge lyfe, perfyte blysse & excedynge plessyre [pleasure], for the mortall eye hath not sene, ne eere [ear] herde, ne mannys herte understode clerly and perfytly how moche clernesse, how moche Joye, how moche swetnes we shall have in that blessyd syghte whan we shall beholde face to face Him that is the lyght of all bryghte thynge, the refuge and reste of travelers & labourers, the receyver and keper of them that torne to Him, the very lyfe to all that lyve, and the crowne of theym that overcome theyre goostly [spiritual] enmyes. Thus I fynde in my soule the ymage of the hygh & gloryous Trynyte, to the whiche moost hyghe & gloryous Trynyte I owe [ought] to referre and orther [order] all my lyfe, that I maye remembre Hym and putte my playsyre & contemplacyon in Hym. The soule is the ymage of almyghty God the whiche conteyneth thre thynges, the mynde, the understondynge, & wyl. To the mynde we attrybute & put all thynge that we lerne or know though we thynke not alway theron. To the understondynge we attrybute all that we knowe is true, the whiche also we commende & putte to our mynde. By the mynde we ben resemblyd & lyke to the Fader, by understondynge to the Sone, & by wyll or love to the Holy Goost, for there is no thynge in us more lyke to the Holy Goost than is the wyll, or so precyous that there is noo gefte [gift] of God, and it is true love, for true love is the gefte of God more noble & excellente than it is, for true love that cometh of God, and is God Himself, is properly called the Holy Goost by whome the love of God is diffused & sprad [spread] in our hertes, and by whome all the holy & blessyd Trynyte dwelleth and abydeth in us.

---

[6] Wynkyn de Worde's translation here reads "Sothly he is both in us and in us," but this is clearly a mistranslation of the Latin.

E. Anonymous, *Tractatus de interiori domo, seu de conscientia ædificanda*, Migne, *PL*
vol. 184, col. 511a–b (compare *Wisdom*, lines 213–18)

Like the *Meditationes*, this treatise on the conscience was attributed during the Middle
Ages both to St. Bernard and to Hugh of St. Victor, though it is probably not by either one
of them. *Wisdom*'s author used it as a source for his description of Will.

Nam inter omnia Dei dona, quae ad salutem hominis spectare videntur, primum et principale bonum, bona voluntas esse cognoscitur, per quam imago similitudinis Dei in nobis
reparatur. Primum est, quia a bona voluntate bonum omne inchoatur. Principale est,
quoniam bona voluntate nihil hominibus utilius datur. Quidquid homo facit, bonum esse
non potest, nisi ex bona voluntate procedat. Sine bona voluntate omnino salvari quispiam
non potest: cum bona voluntate nemo perire potest. Voluntas bona nec dari potest invito,
nec auferri nisi volenti. Voluntas hominis est potestas Dei. Voluntas hominis est, quia velle
in voluntate hominis est; et ideo totum meritum in voluntate est. Quantum vis, tantum
mereris. Quantum crescit voluntas tua bona, tantum crescit meritum tuum. Fac igitur
magnam bonam voluntatem tuam, si vis habere magnum meritum.

For among all the gifts of God that appear to be directed towards man's salvation, the first
and principal is known to be a good will, through which the image of God's likeness is
restored in us. It is first because everything good begins from a good will. It is principal,
since nothing is given more useful to men than a good will. Whatever a man does cannot be
good unless it proceeds from a good will. It is completely impossible for anyone to be saved
without a good will; with a good will, no one can perish. Good will cannot be given to
anyone against their will, nor can it be taken away unless they wish it. The will of man is the
power of God. It is the will of man, because wishing rests in a man's will, and for this reason
all merit is in the will. As much as you wish, so much you deserve. As your good will grows,
so does your merit. Therefore make your good will great, if you wish to have great merit.

F. St. Bonaventure's *Soliloquies* [7]

The *Soliloquies* of St. Bonaventure are in themselves strongly dramatic, consisting of a
dialogue between man (Homo) and his soul (Anima).

Opera omnia, vol. 8, p. 42 (compare *Wisdom* lines 309–23)
Anima: Eia, mi Domine Deus, quantum ego infelix et misera diligere debeo Deum meum,
qui me creavit, cum non eram; redemit, cum perieram, et de multis periculis liberavit me;
quando errabam, reduxit me; quando ignorabam, docuit me; quando peccabam, corripuit
me; quando contristabar, consolatus est me; quando iam pene desperabam, confortavit me;
quando steti, tenuit me; quando cecidi, erexit me; quando ivi, duxit me; quando veni,
suscepit me.

Soul: Woe to me, my Lord God, how much ought I, unhappy and wretched, to love my God,
who created me when I did not exist, who redeemed me when I had perished, and freed me

---

[7] Excerpted from A. Lauer's edition.

from many perils; when I strayed, he brought me back; when I was ignorant, he taught me; when I sinned, he corrected me; when I was sad, he consoled me; when I was on the point of despair, he comforted me; when I stood, he held me; when I fell, he lifted me up; when I went, he led me; when I came, he received me.

OPERA OMNIA, VOL. 8, P. 41 (compare *Wisdom* lines 1106–10):
[Homo:] Revertere adhuc, o anima, Christus in cruce te expectans habet caput inclinatum ad te deosculandam, habet brachia extensa ad te amplexandam, manus apertas ad remunderandum, corpus extensum ad se totum impendendum, pedes affixos ad commanendum, latus apertum ad te in illud intromittendum. Esto ergo, o anima, iam columba nidificans in foraminibus petrae. . . . Haec Bernardus.

Yet return, O Soul, Christ is waiting for you on the Cross. His head is bent down to kiss you, his arms are stretched out to embrace you, his hands are open to forgive, his body is stretched out to hand himself over entirely, his feet are fixed in order to remain with you, his side is open for you to enter into it. O soul, be now a dove building her nest in the openings of the rock. . . . This [is the end of the quotation from] Bernard.

G. *THE NINE THINGS WHICH PLEASE CHRIST / NOVEM VIRTUTES,* CAMBRIDGE, GONVILLE AND CAIUS COLLEGE, MS 140/80, PP. 132–35 (COMPARE *WISDOM*, LINES 998–1065)

This anonymous text survives in both English and Latin versions. Horstmann printed several English versions, both in prose and in verse but, as Smart pointed out, the Latin text contained in Gonville and Caius College MS 140/80 is closer to the *Wisdom* text than any of the English versions.[8] An excerpted text is given here from that manuscript, since the *Wisdom* playwright ignores the lengthy commentary which accompanies each of the "points."

Hic continentur novem virtutes quas Dominus noster Jesus Christus cuidam sancto viro volenti deo servire necnon devote facere que placent ore suo revelavit sibi dicens primo, "Da pauperibus meis unum denarium in vita tua quia mihi hoc plus placet quam si dedisses post vitam tuam montes aureos in monetam compositos." . . .
Secunda virtus. Emitte unam lacrimam pro peccatis tuis et pro amore meo sive passione mea et hoc plus placet mihi quam si plorares tantam aquam quanta continentur in mari pro rebus mundanis . . . Casiodorus . . . ait, "Fletus est cibus animarum coroboracio sensuum absolucio peccatorum refeccio mencium lavacrum culparum. . . .
Tercia virtus. Sustine dulciter et pacienter unum verbum durum et probosum de proximo tuo et magis mihi placet quam si disciplinares corpus tuum cum tot virgis quot possunt crescere super unam arborem vel dietam terre. . . .
Quartus gradus. Vigila una hora pro me et cicius placebit mihi quam si mitteres ultra mare duodecim milites sepulcrum meum vindicaturos. . . .
Quinta virtus. Habeas pietatem et compassionem de proximo tuo inope vel infirmo et hoc enim frequencius mihi placet quam si jejunares xl annis qualibet ebdomada per tres dies in pane et aqua. . . .

---

[8] C. Horstmann, *Yorkshire Writers,* prose texts vol. 1, pp. 110–12; verse text vol. 2, pp. 455–56; Smart, *Some English and Latin Sources and Parallels,* pp. 34–35.

Sexta virtus. Ne dicas sermonem tradiciosum vel fraudulentum de proximo tuo set taceas pro amore meo et amplius mihi placet quam si ambulares per viam nudis plantis quod cursus sanguinis sequeretur vestigia pedum tuorum. . . .

Septima virtus. Ne instiges nec excites proximum tuum ad malum set omnia convertas in meliora et hoc mihi placet quam si semel in die ascendens in celum. . . .

Octava virtus. Frequenter desideres et interroges me et hoc mihi plus placet quam si mater mea et omnes sancti orarent pro te. . . .

Nona virtus. Diligas me solum super omnia et hoc mihi plus placet quam si ascenderes unam columpnam plenam novaculis acutis ita quod caro tua scineretur in particulas irrecuperabiliter in futurum. . . . Item Gregorius in Pastoralibus ait, "Nichil est preciosius deo virtute dileccionis." . . .

Here are the nine virtues which our Lord Jesus Christ revealed by his mouth to a certain holy man who wished to serve God and do piously what pleases Him, saying first, "Give a penny to my poor during your life; that pleases me more than if you were to give mounds of gold coins after your death." . . .

Second virtue. Shed a tear for your sins and for my love or my passion and that pleases me more than if you were to weep as much water as is contained in the sea for worldly things. . . . Cassiodorus . . . says, "Weeping is food for the soul, a strengthening of the senses, a release from sins, a sustenance for the mind, and a washing away of guilt." . . .

Third virtue. Endure calmly and patiently a hard and abusive word from your neighbor and that pleases me more than if you were to discipline your body with as many rods as might grow on a tree or within a day's journey. . . .

Fourth degree. Watch one hour for me and that will please me more than if you were to send twelve avenging soldiers across the sea to my sepulcher. . . .

Fifth virtue. Have pity and compassion on your needy and sick neighbor and that pleases me more than if you were to fast three days in each week for forty years on bread and water . . . .

Sixth virtue. Do not say hateful or false things about your neighbor, but be silent for my love and that pleases me more than if you were to walk on the road with bare feet until a track of blood followed the trail of your feet. . . .

Seventh virtue. Do not incite or press your neighbor to evil, but turn everything to good, and that pleases me more than if on that same day you ascended to heaven. . . .

Eighth virtue. Ask of me and pray to me often, and that pleases me more than if my mother and all the saints prayed for you. . . .

Ninth virtue. Love me alone above all things, and that pleases me more than if you were to climb a pillar set with sharp razors so that your flesh was torn apart into small pieces which could not be joined together again. . . . Note: Gregory, in his "Pastoral Care" says, "Nothing is so precious to God as the love of virtue." . . .

 APPENDIX 2: MUSIC

MUSIC IN *THE PRIDE OF LIFE*

The only explicit indication of music in *The Pride of Life* is the direction that the king's messenger, Mirth, sing a song (line 322, s.d.) as he takes the queen's message to the bishop, perhaps moving from one scaffold or stage to another. The dramatic situation only requires that the song mirror Mirth's high spirits. Very few secular songs survive from the later fourteenth century, but one possibility would be the popular song "*L'homme armé,*" which appears in a variety of polyphonic settings. These all date from later in the fifteenth century, but the tune itself is likely to have been significantly older. There is no reason why the messenger should not sing a song in French, though it is not certain that the tune was known in England.

MUSIC IN *WISDOM*

The stage directions of *Wisdom* specify an unusually extensive use of music, utilizing plainchant, secular polyphony, and dance music. Since in some cases the chant is sung by five or six people, there is also the possibility that some of the liturgical texts might have been sung in polyphonic versions. This appendix provides the music for the relevant chants in the Sarum usage, as well (in two cases) as polyphonic settings of the sort which might have been used.[1]

THE LITURGICAL MUSIC

The most likely source for the liturgical texts which are sung in the play would be the monophonic plainchant of the Sarum rite, which was instituted under the guidance of St. Osmund, who became bishop of Salisbury (Sarum) in 1078 and which remained the primary liturgical usage in the south of England until the Reformation.[2]

---

[1] Richard Rastall notes that since some of the costuming directions in the text (notably Anima's black-on-white dress) may indicate a Dominican connection, it is possible that the music for these chants would have been drawn from Dominican, rather than Sarum, sources (*Minstrels Playing*, p. 459). See also pp. 451–64 for a thorough discussion of the music in the play.

[2] A facsimile of Richard Pynson's 1502 printing of the Sarum processional is published in *Use of Sarum* I.

The processional antiphon "*Nigra sum*" (line164, s.d.) with which the Five Wits enter is given in two versions: a chant and a three-part setting.[3] The text is from Canticles1:4, which does not appear in the liturgy, so I have set it to a suitable psalm tone.[4] If the chant version is used, it would be appropriate for Anima to sing the first line as an intonation (as Rastall suggests), the Five Wits joining her on the words "filia Jerusalem."

The processional antiphon which ends the first section of the play, "*Tota pulcra es*" (line 324, s.d.), is given here both in its Sarum form and in a three-part setting by Forest from the Trent manuscripts.[5] This collection of sacred music was compiled between about 1415 and 1421, so this setting may be a bit too early for the play. It is important to note here that the text is not one of the Marian antiphons beginning "*Tota pulcra es Maria*," but is derived from Canticles 4:7–11 and 2:11–13.

The two verses which Anima sings processionally "in the most lamentabull wyse" (line 996, s.d.) as she and the Mights leave the stage to receive penance are both from the Lamentations of Jeremiah, and thus both appear in the Easter liturgy; the first, "*Magna velud mare contricio*" at matins on Good Friday; the second, "*Plorans ploravit*" at matins on Maundy Thursday the day before. Since they come from two different services, it is not clear how the two verses would be sung, but the two most likely possibilities are either that the verses would have been extracted from the larger settings of the Lamentations and sung successively, or that a newly-composed setting would have been made. I have given the chants for the two verses as they appear in the Easter liturgy and have made minor adjustments to the music to reflect minor differences in wording between the Sarum chant and the playtext.

The antiphon "*Quid retribuam*" with which Anima, her Five Wits, and her three Mights return to the stage transfigured (line 1064, s.d.) is also given in two versions. Since only the second verse, "*Calicem salutaris*," appears in the Sarum use I have followed Rastall's suggestion that the first verse simply be set to the same music.[6] The alternative three-part version is simply a setting of the chant in faubourdon style. The parallel harmonies of faubourdon represent one possible method of elevating the solemnity of an occasion, and thus would be appropriate for the final return of Anima and her retinue.

THE THREE-MEN'S SONG

Secular songs for three men's voices (treble, mean, and tenor) become relatively common towards the end of the fifteenth century, and proliferate in the sixteenth. They appear with some frequency in plays; the best known are the two songs in the Coventry Shearmen and Tailor's Play, the well-known Coventry Carol and the Shepherds' Song.[7] At least some of the

---

[3] The three-part setting in late fifteenth-century style is by Andrea Budgey, of the medieval ensemble *Sine Nomine*.

[4] Tone 1 for Psalm 110, *Liber Usualis* 133.

[5] The Sarum version is taken from *Processionale ad usum Sarum* (Pynson, 1502), fols. 123v–124; the Trent version is in R. von Ficker, ed., *Sieben Trienter Codices VI*, p. 80. Forest's first name is unknown.

[6] Rastall, *Minstrels Playing*, p. 461.

[7] Rastall, *Heaven Singing*, pp. 66–71; *Minstrels Playing*, p. 185.

three-part songs collected by Thomas Ravenscroft appear to have had dramatic connections.[8] The anonymous three-part song given here has the bawdy quality that seems to be demanded by the play; it also has the advantage that the polyphonic setting of the second and third verse parodies the faubourdon style which was often used in a contemporary liturgical context.[9] The tune appears in a five-part setting in the Henry VIII manuscript (British Library Add. 31922, fols. 106v–107r) with the words "And [If] I were a maiden, as many one is . . ."[10] I have extracted the preexisting tune from the tenor part and reset it to a text based loosely on the fifteenth-century secular lyric, "I have a gentil cok."[11]

THE DANCES

I have not given music for the dances. The sources which survive for English dance music at the end of the fifteenth century are very slim, and the largest single collection, the dances from Gresley Hall, Derbyshire, do not fit the instruments specified in the playtext.[12] The stage directions indicate the instruments for each of the three dances: trumpets for Mind's dance of maintenance, a bagpipe for Understanding's jurors, and a hornpipe for Will's dance of lechery. There is no indication of how many trumpets accompany the first dance, but clearly the other two dances use only a single instrument. The Gresley dances, like much other dance music from the period, require at least two players, since they consist of an elaborate (often improvised) treble played over a preexisting tenor. In the case of many dances, including those of the Gresley collection, it is only this tenor part which survives, with the expectation that one or more parts would be improvised above it. The most extensive sources for monophonic dances are Italian, and Jennifer Nevile has suggested that Italian dances may not have been unknown in late fifteenth-century England.[13] If this solution is adopted, the most useful source for both music and choreography is the 1463 dance treatise of Guglielmo Ebreo of Pesaro.[14]

---

[8] *Pammelia* (London, 1609; STC 20759) contains three songs from Beaumont's *Knight of the Burning Pestle*; *Deuteromelia* (London, 1609; STC 20757) contains a further song from the same play, as well as songs from Shakespeare's *Twelfth Night* and Marston's *Jack Drum's Entertainment*; *Melismata* (London, 1611; STC 20758) is a collection of humorous "city" and "country" songs, many of which may have dramatic connections.

[9] The faubourdon setting of the tune is by Garry Crighton of the University of Münster.

[10] Stevens, *Music at the Court of Henry VIII*, pp. 78–79.

[11] The full text of the poem may be found in Salisbury, *Trials and Joys of Marriage*, p. 253.

[12] Fallows, "Gresley Dance Collection, c. 1500."

[13] Nevile, "Dance in Early Tudor England."

[14] Guglielmo Ebreo of Pesaro, *De pratica seu arte tripudii*.

A POSSIBLE SONG FOR NUNCIUS, LINE 322S.D.

L'hom - me, l'hom - me, l'hom - me_ar - mé, l'hom - me_ar - mé, l'hom - me_arm - é doigt - on doub -

ter. Et l'hom - me_ar - mé. On a fait par - tout cri - er, 'A l'as - sault!' D'un hau - bre - gon de

fer. L'hom - me, l'homme, l'hom me_armé, l'hom me_armé, l'hom me_arm - é doigt-on doub - ter.

TO LINE 164, "NIGRA SUM SED FORMOSA," CHANT VERSION

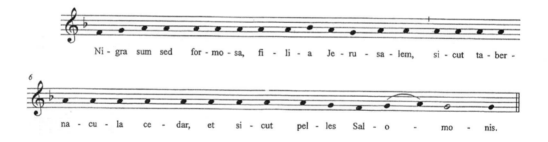

Ni - gra sum sed for - mo - sa, fi - li - a Je - ru - sa - lem, si - cut ta - ber -

na - cu - la ce - dar, et si - cut pel - les Sal - o - mo - nis.

TO LINE 164, "NIGRA SUM SED FORMOSA," POLYPHONIC VERSION

Andrea Budgey

TO LINE 324S.D., "TOTA PULCHRA ES," CHANT VERSION

To line 324s.d., "Tota pulchra es," polyphonic version

Forest

TO LINE 619S.D., SONG FOR MIND, WILL, AND UNDERSTANDING

TO LINE 995, "MAGNA VELUD MARE CONTRICIO"

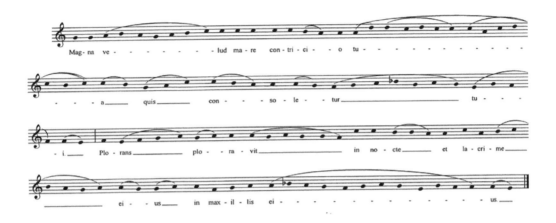

TO LINE 1065S.D., "QUID RETRIBUAM DOMINO," CHANT VERSION

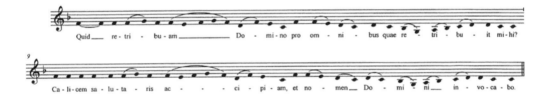

To line 1065s.d., "Quid retribuam Domino," faubourdon version

BIBLIOGRAPHY

"The Abuses of the Age." In *Queene Elizabethes Achademy, etc.* Ed. F. J. Furnivall. EETS e.s. 8. London: Trübner, 1869. P. 88.

Baker, D. C., J. L. Murphy, and L. B. Hall, Jr., eds. *The Late Medieval Religious Plays of Bodleian MSS Digby 133 and E. Museo 160.* EETS o.s. 283. Oxford: Oxford University Press, 1982.

Beadle, Richard, ed. *The Cambridge Companion to Medieval English Theatre.* Cambridge: Cambridge University Press, 1994.

Bennett, Josephine Waters. "The Mediaeval Loveday." *Speculum* 33 (1958), 351–70.

Bevington, David. *From 'Mankind' to Marlowe: The Growth of Structure in the Popular Drama of Tudor England.* Cambridge, MA: Harvard University Press, 1962.

———. "Political Satire in the Morality *Wisdom Who Is Christ.*" *Renaissance Papers* (1964), 41–51.

———. *Tudor Drama and Politics.* Cambridge, MA: Harvard University Press, 1968.

———, ed. *The Macro Plays: A Facsimile Edition with Facing Transcription.* New York: Johnson Reprint, 1972.

———. "*Castles* in the Air: The Morality Plays." In *The Theatre of Medieval Europe: New Research in Early Drama.* Ed. Eckehard Simon. Cambridge: Cambridge University Press, 1986. Pp. 97–116.

Bonaventure. *Soliloquies.* In *Opera omnia.* Vol. 8. Ed. A. Lauer. Florence: Quaracchi, 1898. Pp. 28–67.

Brown, Pamela A., and Peter Parolin, eds. *Women Players in England, 1500–1660: Beyond the All-Male Stage.* Aldershot: Ashgate, 2005.

Clark, Marlene, Sharon Kraus, and Pamela Sheingorn. "'Se in what stat thou doyst indwell': The Shifting Constructions of Gender and Power Relations in *Wisdom.*" In *The Performance of Middle English Culture: Essays on Chaucer and the Drama in Honor of Martin Stevens.* Ed. James J. Paxson, Lawrence M. Clopper, and Sylvia Tomasch. Cambridge: D. S. Brewer, 1998. Pp. 43–57.

Coldewey, John, ed. *Early English Drama: An Anthology.* New York: Garland, 1993.

Craik, T. W. *The Tudor Interlude: Stage, Costume, and Acting.* Leicester: Leicester University Press, 1958.

Davenport, W. A. *Fifteenth-century English Drama: The Early Moral Plays and their Literary Relations.* Cambridge: D. S. Brewer, 1982.

Davidson, Clifford. *Visualizing the Moral Life: Medieval Iconography and the Macro Morality Plays.* New York: AMS Press, 1989.

Davis, Norman, ed. *Non-Cycle Plays and Fragments.* EETS s.s. 1. London: Oxford University Press, 1970.

———. *Non-Cycle Plays and the Winchester Dialogues.* Leeds: Leeds University Press, 1979.

Dean, James M, ed. *Medieval English Political Writings.* Kalamazoo, MI: Medieval Institute Publications, 1996.

Doyle, A. I., ed. *The Vernon Manuscript: A Facsimile of Bodleian Library MS. Eng.poet.a.1.* Woodbridge: D. S. Brewer, 1987.

Eccles, Mark, ed. *The Macro Plays.* EETS o.s. 262. London: Oxford University Press, 1969.

Fallows, David. "The Gresley Dance Collection, c. 1500." *Royal Musical Association Research Chronicle* 29 (1996), 1–20.

Fifield, Merle. "The Use of Doubling and 'Extras' in *Wisdom, Who Is Christ.*" *Ball State University Forum* 6.3 (1965), 65–68.

Fletcher, Alan J. *Drama, Performance, and Polity in Pre-Cromwellian Ireland.* Toronto: University of Toronto Press, 2000. [Especially pp. 82–90.]

Gatch, Milton McC. "Mysticism and Satire in the Morality of *Wisdom*." *Philological Quarterly* 53 (1974), 342–62.

Gesta Romanorum. Ed. S. Herrtage. EETS e.s. 33. London: Oxford University Press, 1896.

Gibson, Gail McMurray. "The Play of *Wisdom* and the Abbey of St. Edmunds." In Riggio, ed., *"Wisdom" Symposium.* Pp. 39–66.

———. *The Theater of Devotion: East Anglian Drama and Society in the Late Middle Ages.* Chicago: University of Chicago Press, 1989.

Gower, John. *Confessio Amantis.* Ed. Russell A. Peck. 3 vols. Kalamazoo, MI: Medieval Institute Publications, 2002–06.

Guglielmo Ebreo of Pesaro. *"De pratica seu arte tripudii." On the practice or art of dancing.* Ed. and trans. Barbara Sparti. Poems trans. Michael Sullivan. Oxford: Clarendon Press, 1993.

Happé, Peter, ed. *Tudor Interludes.* Harmondsworth: Penguin, 1972.

Harrison, William. *The Description of England: The Classic Contemporary Account of Tudor Social Life.* Ed. Georges Edelen. Ithaca, NY: Cornell University Press, 1968.

Hengstebeck, Irmlind. "Wer träumt in *The Pride of Life*?" *Archiv für das Studium der Neueren Sprachen und Literaturen* 208 (1972), 120–22.

Hill, Eugene D. "The Trinitarian Allegory of the Moral Play of *Wisdom*." *Modern Philology* 73 (1975), 121–35.

Hilton, Walter. *Walter Hilton's Mixed Life Edited from Lambeth Palace MS 472.* Ed. S. J. Ogilvie-Thompson. Salzburg: Institut für Anglistik und Amerikanistik, 1986.

———. *The Scale of Perfection.* Ed. Thomas H. Bestul. Kalamazoo, MI: Medieval Institute Publications, 2000.

Horstmann, C., ed. *Yorkshire Writers: Richard Rolle of Hampole, an English Father of the Church, and His Followers.* 2 vols. London: Swan Sonnenschein, 1895–96. [Especially vol. 1, pp 264–92.]

Horstmann, K. "*Orologium Sapientiae*, or *The Seven Poyntes of Trewe Wisdom*, aus ms. Douce 114." *Anglia* 10 (1888), 323–89.

The Hours of Etienne Chevalier. New York: G. Braziller, 1971.

James, M. R., trans. *The Apocryphal New Testament.* Oxford: Clarendon Press, 1924.

Johnston, Alexandra F. "*Wisdom* and the Records: Is There a Moral?" In Riggio, ed., *"Wisdom" Symposium.* Pp. 87–102.

———. "The Audience of the English Moral Play." *Fifteenth Century Studies* 13 (1988), 291–97.

———. "Parish Playmaking before the Reformation." In *The Late Medieval Parish.* Ed. Clive Burgess and Eamon Duffy. Donington: Tyas and Watkins, 2006. Pp. 322–38.

Jones, Marion. "Early Moral Plays and the Earliest Secular Drama." In *Medieval Drama.* Ed. A. C. Cawley, Marion Jones, Peter F. McDonald, and David Mills. *The Revels History of Drama in English*, vol. 1. London: Methuen, 1983. Pp. 213–91.

Katzenellenbogen, Adolf. *Allegories of the Virtues and Vices in Medieval Art: From Early Christian Times to the Thirteenth Century.* Toronto: University of Toronto Press, 1989.

Kelley, Michael R. *Flamboyant Drama: A Study of The Castle of Perseverance, Mankind, and Wisdom.* Carbondale: Southern Illinois University Press, 1979.

Kim, H. C., ed. *The Gospel of Nichodemus.* Toronto: Pontifical Institute of Mediaeval Studies, 1973.

King, Pamela M. "Morality Plays." In Beadle. Pp. 240–64.

Klausner, David N. "The Modular Structure of *Wisdom*." In *Bring Furth the Pagants: Essays in Early English Drama Presented to Alexandra F. Johnston.* Ed. David N. Klausner and Karen S. Marsalek. Toronto: University of Toronto Press, 2006. Pp. 181–96.

Koontz, Christian. "The Duality of Styles in the Morality Play *Wisdom Who Is Christ*: A Classical-Rhetorical Analysis." *Style* 7 (1973), 251–70.

Lancashire, Ian, ed. *Two Tudor Interludes: Youth and Hick Scorner.* Manchester: Manchester University Press, 1980.

Love, Nicholas. *The Mirror of the Blessed Life of Jesus Christ*. Ed. Michael G. Sargent. Exeter: University of Exeter Press, 2004.

MacKenzie, W. Roy. *The English Moralities from the Point of View of Allegory*. Boston: Ginn, 1914.

Marshall, John. "Marginal Staging Marks in the Macro Manuscript of *Wisdom*." *Medieval English Theatre* 7.2 (1985), 77–82.

Meditationes piissime de cognitione humanae conditionis (of St. Bernard?). In J. P. Migne, ed., *Patrologia Latina*. Vol. 184, cols. 485a–507b. Trans. Wynkyn de Worde in *The Medytacyens of Saynt Bernarde*. 1496 (STC 1917).

Mills, James, ed. *The Account Roll of the Priory of the Holy Trinity, Dublin, 1337–1346, with the Middle English Moral Play "The Pride of Life."* Dublin: Royal Society of Antiquaries of Ireland, 1891.

Molloy, John Joseph. *A Theological Interpretation of the Moral Play, Wisdom, Who Is Christ*. Washington, DC: Catholic University of America Press, 1952.

Neuss, Paula, ed. *Aspects of Early English Drama*. Cambridge: D. S. Brewer, 1983.

Nevile, Jennifer. "Dance in Early Tudor England: An Italian Connection?" *Early Music* 26 (May 1998), 230–45.

"The Nine Virtues." Gonville and Caius College, Cambridge, MS 140.80, pp. 132–35.

Nisse, Ruth. *Defining Acts: Drama and the Politics of Interpretation in Late Medieval England*. Notre Dame, IN: University of Notre Dame Press, 2005. [Especially chapter 6, "The Mixed Life in Motion: *Wisdom*'s Devotional Politics," pp. 125–48.]

Norland, H. B. *Drama in Early Britain, 1485–1558*. Lincoln: University of Nebraska Press, 1995.

The N-Town Play. Ed. Stephen Spector. 2 vols. EETS s.s. 11–12. Oxford: Oxford University Press, 1991.

Potter, Robert. *The English Morality Play: Origins, History and Influence of a Dramatic Tradition*. London: Routledge & Kegan Paul, 1975.

Preston, Michael. *A Concordance to Four 'Moral' Plays: The Castle of Perseverance, Wisdom, Mankind, and Everyman*. Ann Arbor, MI: University Monographs, 1975.

Pynson, Richard, pub. *Processionale ad usum Sarum*. Ed. R. Rastall. Kilkenny: Boethius Press, 1980.

Rastall, Richard. *The Heaven Singing: Music in Early English Religious Drama*. Vol 1. Cambridge: Boydell & Brewer, 1996.

———. *Minstrels Playing: Music in Early English Religious Drama*. Vol. 2. Cambridge: Boydell & Brewer, 2001. [Chapter 16, "Wisdom," pp. 451–64.]

Riggio, Milla Cozart, ed. *The "Wisdom" Symposium: Papers from the Trinity College Medieval Festival*. New York: AMS Press, 1986.

———. "The Staging of *Wisdom*." In Riggio, ed., *"Wisdom" Symposium*. Pp. 1–17.

———. "*Wisdom* Enthroned: Iconic Stage Portraits." *Comparative Drama* 23 (1989), 228–54.

———, ed. *The Play of Wisdom: Its Texts and Contexts*. New York: AMS Press, 1998.

Salisbury, Eve, ed. *The Trials and Joys of Marriage*. Kalamazoo, MI: Medieval Institute Publications, 2002.

Scherb, Victor I. *Staging Faith: East Anglian Drama in the Later Middle Ages*. London: Associated University Presses, 2001.

Schmitt, Natalie Crohn. "The Idea of a Person in Medieval Morality Plays." *Comparative Drama* 12 (1978), 23–34.

Smart, Walter Kay. *Some English and Latin Sources and Parallels for the Morality of Wisdom*. Menasha, WI: George Banta Publishing, 1912.

Smith, Mary Frances. *Wisdom and Personification of Wisdom Occurring in Middle English Literature before 1500*. Washington, DC: Catholic University of America Press, 1935.

Spivack, Bernard. *Shakespeare and the Allegory of Evil: The History of a Metaphor in Relation to His Major Villains*. New York: Columbia University Press, 1958.

Spivack, Charlotte. "Feminine vs. Masculine in English Morality Drama." *Fifteenth Century Studies* 13 (1988), 137–44.

Stevens, John, ed. *Music at the Court of Henry VIII*. Musica Britannica XVIII. London: Stainer and Bell, 1969.

———. *Early Tudor Songs and Carols*. Musica Britannica XXXVI. London: Stainer and Bell, 1975.

Thomas à Kempis. *De imitatione Christi: Libri quatuor*. Ed. Tiburzio Lupo. Rome: Libreria Editrice Vaticana, 1982.

Tilley, Morris Palmer. *A Dictionary of the Proverbs in England in the Sixteenth and Seventeenth Centuries: A Collection of the Proverbs Found in English Literature and the Dictionaries of the Period*. Ann Arbor: University of Michigan Press, 1966.

Tractatus de interiori domo, seu de conscientia ædificanda. In J. P. Migne, ed. *Patrologia Latina*. Vol. 184, cols. 507c–552c.

Voigts, Linda Ehrsam. "Fifteenth-Century English Banns Advertising the Services of an Itinerant Doctor." In *Between Text and Patient: The Medieval Enterprise in Medieval and Early Modern Europe*. Firenze: Sismel/Edizione del Galluzzo, forthcoming.

von Ficker, Rudolf, ed. *Sieben Trienter Codices VI: Geistliche und weltliche Kompositionen des XIV u XV Jhs*. Denmäler der Tonkunst in Österreich 76. Graz: Akademische Druck und Verlagsanstalt, 1960.

Walker, Greg, ed. *Medieval Drama*. Oxford: Blackwell, 2000.

Wasson, John. "The Morality Play: Ancestor of Elizabethan Drama?" *Comparative Drama* 13 (1979), 210–21.

Wenzel, Siegfried. "The Three Enemies of Man." *Mediaeval Studies* 29 (1968), 47–66.

Westfall, Suzanne. *Patrons and Performance: Early Tudor Household Revels*. Oxford: Clarendon Press, 1990.

Whiting, Bartlett Jere, with the collaboration of Helen Wescott Whiting. *Proverbs, Sentences, and Proverbial Phrases from English Writings Mainly before 1500*. Cambridge, MA: The Belknap Press of Harvard University Press, 1968.

———. *Proverbs in the Earlier English Drama*. New York: Octagon Books, 1969.

Williams, Arnold. "The English Moral Play before 1500." *Annuale Medievale* 4 (1963), 9–12.

Williams, Elijah. *Early Holborn and the Legal Quarter of London: A Topographical Survey of the Beginnings of the District Known as Holborn and of the Inns of Court and of Chancery*. 2 vols. London: Sweet & Maxwell, 1927.

GLOSSARY

The glossary covers the two play texts, but not the source material printed in Appendix 1.

abey, abye *suffer; pay a penalty or fine*
accordyt, acordyt *suits, is appropriate to*
acumberyde *overcame*
afer, afere *frighten*
affyable *agreeable one, lover*
affyance *reliance, dependence*
affye *trust*
aghte *ought*
alend *come, arrive*
als *as*
alyng *altogether*
amis *wrongly, badly*
Amralté *Admiralty*
amyke *beloved*
anosyde *harmed, injured*
anow *enough*
aplye *apply, devote*
applyede *attributed*
apposyde *examined*
aquyt *acquit, release*
aray *costume, clothing*
arere *raise*
arest *arrest*
arome *far off, at a distance, roaming*
aryght *immediately; properly*
aryve *arrive*
aslawe *slain*
aspye *notice, see, find out*
assende *ascend*
assyduly *assiduously, continuously*
asythe *atonement*
atastyde *tasted*
ataunt *in excess*
avaunsyd *promoted*
avaunt, avaunte *brag, boast*

avoydyth *drives out*
ay *always, forever*
ayeins *towards; against*
ay-whan *whenever*

bachelere *young man, knight*
bal, bale *evil, hardship*
baldli *certainly, clearly*
banis *banns, proclamation*
behou *benefit*
behovefulle *appropriate; profitable*
benygnyté *kindness*
beschrew *curse*
beseke *seek*
bet, beth, bethe, bett *are*
beteche *commend to*
bethynke *consider*
betit *beats, overcomes*
betyme *promptly; early*
beyght *bait, enticement, bribe*
bilent (wyt) *come (to)*
bilevyd *neglected*
bisey *careful*
biwent *went, lived*
bled *creature*
blyne *cease*
blyve *quickly, immediately*
bode *threaten*
bolhed *bullhead, idiot*
bore, borre *born*
boun *readily*
bowhede *bowed*
bowr *chamber, private apartment*
bren *brain; brows*
brennynge *burning*

breydest *reproach*
brit *bright*
bronde, brondis, brondys *firebrand,
     torch; sword*
brouke *use*
browys *eyebrows*
burthen *burden*
byght *bite; be severe*

cache *catch*
caren *carrion*
carye *be afraid*
cayser *emperor*
cepman *merchant, tradesman*
chagler *windbag*
cham *came*
chapelettys, chapplettys *coronets,
     small crowns*
char *care*
charp *carp, speak*
chere *behavior, spirit; precious*
cherysyste *cherishes*
cheveler, chevelers *wigs*
cheveleryde *wearing a wig*
chevesaunce *fraud, trick to get money*
chong, chonge, schonge *trade, change*
choppe *bargain*
chorle, chorlys *churl, base person*
chout *knew*
churg *church*
clene *pure, clean, innocent*
clennes *purity, innocence*
clepe, clepyde *call, name*
clere *clearly*
closyde *buried, covered*
clovyn *split*
clumme *silent*
clymyt *climbs*
cognycyon *knowledge*
comly *becoming, appropriate*
complexccyon, compleccyons
     temperament
confyrmacyon *consent*
conregent *with equal authority, ruling
     together; in the same livery*
contenance *masked; with expressive
     gestures*

convenyent *appropriate*
conversant *familiar*
cors *body*
cosyn *relative*
couthe *could*
covetys, covetyse *covetousness*
cowdys *could*
Cresten *Christian*
crestyde *crowned, liveried*
crestys *badges of livery*
crose *head of a coin* (see **pyll**)
cumli *fittingly*
cumlic *handsome*
cure *care*
curtely *courtly*
custume *habit, custom*
custummaly *customarily*

dalyance *play; idle conversation*
dame *mother*
damesellys *maidens*
dammyde *damned*
dasche *strike, hit*
dau (don of dau) *day (put to death)*
daunte *satisfy; tame*
**defoule, defoulyde, defyle,
     dyffoulyde** *defile*
deit *died*
del *control*
delectacyon, dylectacyon *pleasure,
     delight*
delful *terrible, painful*
delith *deals, gives*
demisman *judge*
dere *dear; costly; brave*
derrist *bravest*
desyderable *desirable, longed for*
devoydyth *exits*
devys *heraldic device; person wearing
     livery*
dew, du *due, appropriate*
dispyte *dispute, argue*
dobullnes *duplicity*
doghtely *bravely*
doghti, douti *brave*
dompe, dumme *stupid; silent*
domys *judgments*

dot *dies*
douce *sweet*
dout, doute *fear, doubt*
drawte *drawn out*
dres *decorate, prepare*
dryvande *going*
dur *dares*
dyght *ordain; prepare; put*
dyrke *dark*
dyscheyit *deceit*
dyscrey *perceive*
dysporte *sport*
dysposyde *inclined; spent*
dysprave *slander*
dyspyes *despises*
dyspyght *malice, hatred*
dyspytuusly *insultingly, hatefully*

egalle *equal*
eke *also*
ellys *otherwise*
ending-daws *last days, death*
enduyde *endowed*
endyght *indict, prosecute*
endyn *end, die*
engrose *confiscate, take possession of*
enmy, enmye, enmyes *enemy*
enquer *inquire, ask*
entent *advice, counsel*
entret *entreaty; jury-bribing*
eschew, eschewe *avoid*
espyede *noticed, seen*
eteit *eat*
eveyn-crysten *fellow Christians*
expedyente *useful, appropriate*
expellyt *drives away*
exposycyon *understanding*
expres *for certain, surely*
eye *fear*

fainist *most beautiful*
fale, fel, fele *many*
fay *faith*
fel *skin*
fend, fende, fendis *devil*
ficis *fish*
florresschist *flourish, brandish*

fonde *try*
fondnes *foolishness*
fonnyde *foolish*
fors *consider, regard, think*
fortherers *promoters*
freellnes, freelté *frailty*
fremit *unrelated person*

gaff *gave*
galont, galonte, galontes, galontys
    fashionable young man
gederyde *gathered, assembled*
gees *intend; guess*
geet *get*
geyl *deceit, guile*
gin, ginnith, gyn, gynne *begins*
gird *strike*
gostlic *profoundly; spiritually*
gostly *spiritual*
govell *usury*
gras *grace*
grates *gratitude*
graven *buried*
grete, grett *great*
grisful *terrible*
gronde *ground, basis, foundation*
grou *grieve*
gyedly *splendidly*
gyse *fashion, manner, custom*

hal *all, entirely; hall*
halse *embrace*
halt *hold*
ham *home*
hante *haunt; use*
happe *happen*
har *their*
harlottys *evil persons*
harow *harrow! (cry of distress)*
hattys *hats*
hayer *heir*
he *he; she*
hedyr, hidir, hydir, hydyr *here, in*
    this direction
heelfull *healthy*
hei, hey, hy, hye *high, tall*
hel, hele *health*

hel, helle *hell*
helmis *helmets*
hem *them*
hend, hende *near; gracious; end*
henge *hanged*
hennis, hens *hence*
her *her; here*
hestis, hestys *commands*
hevede *head*
hind *end*
hir *their*
ho *she*
hodys *hoods*
holl *whole*
holly *worship*
holys *holes*
honde *hand*
hoope, hoppe *hope*
hote *command*
hurde *store, hoard*
(y)hyght *was/is called*

ibore, iborre *born*
icom *come*
ifer *together*
ikaghte *caught*
ikorne, ikorre *chosen; famous*
iliche *like*
ilore *lost*
imad *made, created*
inclyne *submit, accept*
induyr *endure*
indwell *inhabit*
infenyt *infinite*
informable *knowledgeable*
inow, inowe *enough*
inperfyghtnes *imperfection*
inspyryt *inspires*
ipocryttys *hypocrites*
irerit *established*
isen *seen*
iustis *justice*
iwis, iwys *indeed, certainly, truly*

jentyll *gentle*
juge-partynge *bribing of judges*

kempis *warriors*
kertyllys *overskirts*
kete *bold*
kinde, kynde *nature*
kith, kyt *shows, manifests*
knett *knit*
knyt, knytis *knight(s)*
korin *chosen*
kynrede *kindred*

lace *wrap*
lafte *left*
lak *find fault (with)*
lanys *lanes, streets*
lasyde *fastened*
lec, leche *doctor*
lecuri *lechery*
leeffull *lawful*
lefe *leaf*
leint *length, height*
lende *participate*
lenust *most lean; most frail*
lere, lerne *learn*
lerit *educated*
lesing, lesynge *lie, falsehood*
lest *least*
lestenith *listen*
lett *allow, leave*
lettrit *educated*
leut *uneducated*
lev, leve *leave*
lever *better (for); rather*
lewyde *uneducated*
leyfte *left*
leynth *length*
lib *live*
lisst *lie*
list, liste *desire, please; am/are bidden*
lombys *lamb's*
lond, londe, londis *land, lands*
lor *wisdom*
lore *lost*
lought *bow down*
lovelich *lovely*
lovevyt, lovit, lovyt, lovyth *loves*
lovynly *lovingly*
lyghtlyer *more easily*

lykly *handsome*
lykynge *happy*
lykyngys *desires*
lynde *linden; lime tree*
lyst *want, desire*
lyvyt *lives*

mac *make*
mad *made*
mafay *by my faith*
maistri, maistrie, maistrye *power, authority*
males *malice*
malewrye *misfortune*
mare *more*
marre *confuse, trouble*
mase *makes, causes*
mastres *mistress*
maynpris *bail*
mayntement *maintenance*
med, mede *earnings, reward; bribery*
medsyne *medicine*
mekyt *makes meek*
mene *complain; mean; middle voice*
mengylde *mixed*
meny, menye, meyn, meyné *retinue, company*
menyver *white fur, ermine*
meroure *mirror*
mest *most*
meth *power, ability*
metis *meets, comes together*
mevynge *action*
miste *missed, omitted*
mit *might*
mitir *miter*
mo *more*
mod, mode *mood; mind*
moder, modyr *mother*
molde *mold; earth*
moque *take pleasure*
mornyth *suffers*
mosyde *deceived*
mot *may*
mout *mouth*
mouyntenys *mountains*
mucil *much, greatly*

munit *warns*
mut *must*
myrable *wonderful*
mys *fail; sin*
mysfare *go wrong*
misst *must*

nas *was not*
nast *have not*
nede *necessary*
nel *will not*
ner *near; not at all*
nere *near*
nesesse *necessary*
nex *next*
ney *nor*
nis *is not*
nit *night*
nobley *nobility*
nold *would not*
nost *know not*
nother, nothir *neither*
notys *musical notes*
nowere *nowhere*
nynte *ninth*
nyse *foolish*
nysyté *foolishness*

obeysance *obedience*
ocke *but*
ofir *over*
onclennes *lechery, filth*
oncunnynge *ignorance*
onis, onys *once*
onkynd, onkynde *unnatural*
onlerit *uneducated*
onthryvande *useless, unprofitable*
onto *unto*
or *before*
ordenance *plan, plot*
ordenyde *ordained, decreed*
ordure *filth, excrement, garbage*
ordynatly *properly*
oreble *horrible*
other *or*
othis *oaths*
ou *you*

ough *owe*
outhe *out*
outwrynge *squeeze out*
ouyr *hour*
ovre *over*
oyein, oyeyne *again*
oyeynis *against*

pacyenly *patiently*
paraventur *perhaps*
parvyse *enclosure at a church door*
passante *stylish, fashionable*
pawsacyon *pause*
peas, pees, pes *peace*
pere *equal*
perlys *pearls*
perrysschyt *destroys*
pervert, perverte *pervert, go astray*
peyn, peyne, peyns, peynys *pain,
     pains*
pleynerly *obviously*
pleyntuus *plentiful*
pol *pool*
pompyus *ostentatious*
povert *poverty*
praty *pretty*
prec, preche *preach*
precyosnes *wealth, richness*
prerogatyff *inherent right*
prest *ready*
preve *prove*
prevynge *proving*
profyght *profit*
prolocutor *speaker*
prowe *profit*
prykkys *spikes, thorns*
purfyled *edged, bordered*
puysschaunce *force*
pyctoure *image*
pyler *pillar*
pyll *tail of a coin* (see **crose**)
pynne *pen, peg*

quak *quake*
quell, qwell *destroy*
quen, qwen *queen*
quytte, qwyte *repay*

rampaunt *(heraldic) standing on hind
     legs in profile*
rast *ease, comfort*
rave *express oneself passionately*
raveyn *plunder, rapine*
rechace *hunting call to muster hounds*
rechase *judicial review*
reclusyde *hidden*
recordaunce *false testifying*
recurable *curable*
recure *reward*
recurythe *obtains legal possession*
reddure *punishment*
rede *advise; red*
reducyde *led back*
reformynge *re-establishing*
regyn *region*
reke *care*
rekleshede *carelessness*
relacyon *account; knowledge*
relessyt, relesyt *releases, frees*
reme *realm*
remene *remember*
ren, renne, rennis, rennyt *run, runs*
rent *torn*
renuyde *restored*
repeyer *turn; resort*
replicacyon *reply*
reprehende *condemn*
repreve *reproof*
reprovable *reprehensible*
resort, resorte *go (for help); retinue*
resythe *rise, lift up*
retenance *retinue*
retornys *writ payments*
reulyde *ruled*
reut, ruthe *pity*
reuthyles *ruthless, pitiless*
reve *deprive*
rewe *regret*
reynge *reign*
reysyst *raise, uplift*
rit *right; very*
ro *roe, female deer*
Rode *Cross*
rot *root; foundation*
route *run riot*

rubbyt *scrubs*
ryghtusnes *righteousness*
ryve *tear apart*

sage *elderly; wise*
satysfye *pay for*
savrit *savored*
savy *save*
schappe *form, appearance; beauty*
schen *shining*
schere *shire, county*
schir *sir*
scho *she*
schonge see **chong**
schrew *curse*
schrewde, schrewede *mischievous, clever*
schullin *shall*
schylyngys *shillings*
sckyppe *skip*
scot *thrown*
screu *shrew, villain*
seker, sekyr, sikir *certain*
sekyrnes *certainty*
sen *seen; sin*
sensyble *perceivable (by the senses)*
sentys, seyntys *saints*
ser *sir*
seth, sethe *since; says*
sew, sewe *lead to, follow*
seyer *lawyer*
shendeschyppe *shameful behavior*
shrew *curse*
sib *relation*
sig, sigge *say, said*
skil *reason; reasonable*
slet, sleye *wise, clever*
sleyght, sleyghtys, sleyttys *trickery*
slyppe *slip, slide*
smartli *quickly*
smert *dies*
smerte *sharp*
soleyn *proud, haughty*
sondis *shore*
sorre *sorely; strongly*
sot, soth, sothe *truth*

soute *sought*
spart, sparye, sparyth *spare*
spec, speche *speech*
specyfye *describe*
sped, spede, spedit *hasten; thrive, succeed*
spelle *story, narrative*
spellys *utters*
spille, spyll, spylle *destroy*
spousebreche *adultery*
spoyll *divest*
stabil, stable *steadfast*
starre *stare, glare*
stere *direct*
sterne *severe, difficult*
sterre *incite, stir*
sterynge, steryngys *stirring; impulse*
stews, stewys *brothels*
stif *steadfast*
stont *stands; exists*
stotey *bravery*
stounde *period of time*
stout, stoute *strong*
streightly *frugally*
streinth, strent, streyint, streynt, streynth, strynt *strength*
strengtheth *strengthens*
streytly *strictly; narrowly*
streytt *limited*
suc *such*
sue *pursue, follow*
sune *son*
sut, sute *livery; matching costumes*
swaynis *men*
swetter *sweeter*
swyn *swine*
swyre *neck*
symony, symonye *simony, buying and selling church offices*
symylytude *image*
syn, syne, synn, synne, synnys *sin; sign*
syngler, synglere *curious; special, individual*
sypres *cypress*
sythe *since*

tal *tale*
talente *intention, desire*
taut *taught*
ten, tene *annoy, anger*
tende *listen to*
tenker *tinker*
tenour *tenor, lowest musical part*
tere *tear*
thede *country*
thedyr *there*
thegh *although*
thingit *think*
thore *there*
thot *though*
thout, thowte *thought*
thrawe *suffer*
threttys *threats*
threys *thrice*
thryfte *prosperity*
thryvande *thriving*
torne *turn*
touart *towards*
trace, traces *dance*
tramposyde *transposed, converted*
tre *wood*
trebull *treble, highest musical part*
trecri *treachery*
trespas *trespass; sin*
treut, treuthe, trouth, trouthe, truyt
    truth
trist, troust *believe, trust*
tristili *faithfully*
trow *think, believe*
trumpes, trumpys *trumpets*
trymbull *tremble*
tyght, tyghte *tight, tightly*
tyng *thing*

uche *each*
unabylythe *makes unfit for, disables*
unclosyde *opened*
unstabullnes *instability*
usance *usage*
usande *being used*

varyance *question; disagreement*
verray *true*

veyne *vain*
victoryall *of victory*
vyseryde *masked*
vysurs *masks*

wan, wen *when*
war, wer *where*
ware *beware*
warnit *warns*
wat, watt *what*
wede *clothing*
wedys *weeds*
welde *control*
wend, wende *go, turn*
wene *think, believe; understand*
werre *war*
wet, wete *know*
whow, whowe *how!* (?)
wight, wyght *white; creature, person*
wirch *work; cause*
wittin *know*
wo, woo *who; harm, woe*
wode, wood, woode *mad, insane*
wom *whom*
wondyde *wounded*
wonschildis *defenders*
wordly *worldly, secular*
wore *were*
wosa, woso *whoso*
wot, wote, wott *knows*
wrake *ruin*
wreist *anger*
wrother *evil, disastrous*
wroute *created*
wrye *conceal*
wy *why*
wyc, wyche *which*
wyke *week*
wyly *wily, clever*
wynke *sleep*
wynnande *winning*
wyppe *quick!* (?)
wyrre *hurry!* (?)
wyrry *throat*
wyt *with; knowledge*
wyvande *wived, married*

yar *ready*
yche *each*
yeff, yeve, yiue *give*
yeftys, yiffte *gifts*
yelpe, yilp, yilpe *speak well, praise;*
    boast

ynowe *enough*
yomandrye *yeomanry, retinue*
yougthe *youth*
yove *given*
yyng *young*

✒ MIDDLE ENGLISH TEXTS SERIES

William Dunbar, *The Complete Works*, edited by John Conlee (2004)

Chaucerian Dream Visions and Complaints, edited by Dana M. Symons (2004)

Stanzaic Guy of Warwick, edited by Alison Wiggins (2004)

Saints' Lives in Middle English Collections, edited by E. Gordon Whatley, with Anne B. Thompson and Robert K. Upchurch (2004)

Siege of Jerusalem, edited by Michael Livingston (2004)

The Kingis Quair and Other Prison Poems, edited by Linne R. Mooney and Mary-Jo Arn (2005)

The Chaucerian Apocrypha: A Selection, edited by Kathleen Forni (2005)

John Gower, *The Minor Latin Works*, edited and translated by R. F. Yeager, with *In Praise of Peace*, edited by Michael Livingston (2005)

Sentimental and Humorous Romances: Floris and Blancheflour, Sir Degrevant, The Squire of Low Degree, The Tournament of Tottenham, and The Feast of Tottenham, edited by Erik Kooper (2006)

The Dicts and Sayings of the Philosophers, edited by John William Sutton (2006)

"Everyman" and Its Dutch Original, "Elckerlijc," edited by Clifford Davidson, Martin W. Walsh, and Ton J. Broos (2007)

The N-Town Plays, edited by Douglas Sugano, with assistance by Victor I. Scherb (2007)

The Book of John Mandeville, edited by Tamarah Kohanski and C. David Benson (2007)

John Lydgate, *The Temple of Glas*, edited by J. Allan Mitchell (2007)

The Northern Homily Cycle, edited by Anne B. Thompson (2008)

Codex Ashmole 61: A Compilation of Popular Middle English Verse, edited by George Shuffelton (2008)

Chaucer and the Poems of "Ch," edited by James I. Wimsatt (revised edition 2009)

William Caxton, *The Game and Playe of the Chesse*, edited by Jenny Adams (2009)

John the Blind Audelay, *Poems and Carols*, edited by Susanna Fein (2009)

COMMENTARY SERIES

Haimo of Auxerre, *Commentary on the Book of Jonah*, translated with an introduction and notes by Deborah Everhart (1993)

Medieval Exegesis in Translation: Commentaries on the Book of Ruth, translated with an introduction and notes by Lesley Smith (1996)

Nicholas of Lyra's Apocalypse Commentary, translated with an introduction and notes by Philip D. W. Krey (1997)

Rabbi Ezra Ben Solomon of Gerona, *Commentary on the Song of Songs and Other Kabbalistic Commentaries*, selected, translated, and annotated by Seth Brody (1999)

John Wyclif, *On the Truth of Holy Scripture*, translated with an introduction and notes by Ian Christopher Levy (2001)

Second Thessalonians: Two Early Medieval Apocalyptic Commentaries, introduced and translated by Steven R. Cartwright and Kevin L. Hughes (2001)

The "Glossa Ordinaria" on the Song of Songs, translated with an introduction and notes by Mary Dove (2004)

DOCUMENTS OF PRACTICE SERIES

Love and Marriage in Late Medieval London, selected, translated, and introduced by Shannon McSheffrey (1995)

Sources for the History of Medicine in Late Medieval England, selected, introduced, and translated by Carole Rawcliffe (1995)

A Slice of Life: Selected Documents of Medieval English Peasant Experience, edited, translated, and with an introduction by Edwin Brezette DeWindt (1996)

Regular Life: Monastic, Canonical, and Mendicant "Rules," selected and introduced by Douglas J. McMillan and Kathryn Smith Fladenmuller (1997); second edition, selected and introduced by Daniel Marcel La Corte and Douglas J. McMillan (2004)

Women and Monasticism in Medieval Europe: Sisters and Patrons of the Cistercian Reform, selected, translated, and with an introduction by Constance H. Berman (2002)

Medieval Notaries and Their Acts: The 1327–1328 Register of Jean Holanie, introduced, edited, and translated by Kathryn L. Reyerson and Debra A. Salata (2004)

✒ MEDIEVAL GERMAN TEXTS IN BILINGUAL EDITIONS SERIES

Sovereignty and Salvation in the Vernacular, 1050–1150, introduction, translations, and notes by James A. Schultz (2000)

Ava's New Testament Narratives: "When the Old Law Passed Away," introduction, translation, and notes by James A. Rushing, Jr. (2003)

History as Literature: German World Chronicles of the Thirteenth Century in Verse, introduction, translation, and notes by R. Graeme Dunphy (2003)

✒ VARIA

The Study of Chivalry: Resources and Approaches, edited by Howell Chickering and Thomas H. Seiler (1988)

Studies in the Harley Manuscript: The Scribes, Contents, and Social Contexts of British Library MS Harley 2253, edited by Susanna Fein (2000)

The Liturgy of the Medieval Church, edited by Thomas J. Heffernan and E. Ann Matter (2001; second edition 2005)

✒ TO ORDER PLEASE CONTACT:

Medieval Institute Publications
Western Michigan University
Kalamazoo, MI 49008-5432
Phone (269) 387-8755
FAX (269) 387-8750
http://www.wmich.edu/medieval/mip/index.html

Typeset in 10/13 New Baskerville
and Golden Cockerel Ornaments display
Designed by Linda K. Judy
Manufactured by Cushing-Malloy, Inc.

Medieval Institute Publications
College of Arts and Sciences
Western Michigan University
1903 W. Michigan Avenue
Kalamazoo, MI 49008-5432
http:/ /www.wmich.edu/medieval/mip

 WESTERN MICHIGAN UNIVERSITY